Praise for

"When the stakes are high, ~~you can't possibly~~ succeed without extraordinary leadership. The future belongs to the skilled leaders who evolve to remain relevant, who are human-centric, influential, innovative and adaptable... this is Lead Beyond 2030."

Sadhana Smiles
Chief Executive Officer, Harcourts Victoria & REIP

"Caroline Kennedy has given us so much intelligence, experience and wisdom here. She's walked the path of executive leadership as a CEO. Grounded in research and practical experience, this book is for every leader who wants to make a real, long-lasting difference. An invaluable tool for rethinking leadership and remaining relevant."

Prashant Billimoria
Chief Operating Officer, Workwear Group

"Caroline Kennedy takes us on a thought-provoking journey to realise that what worked in the past won't work tomorrow. Transformational leadership is often more about unlearning than learning; her to-the-point writing style challenges you to cast aside traditional ideas of role models and behaviours. *Lead Beyond 2030* is a force multiplier for anyone who doesn't want to get left behind."

Andrew Oxley
Managing Director, Integral Group

"The business landscape is in a cycle of continuous change, in the last decade the turbulent conditions have forced leaders to operate at hyper speed with a focus on the short to medium term. Caroline Kennedy provides compelling insights into the criticality of self-examination and self-reflection. She supplies tangible examples of the skills that a leader at the helm will need in order to navigate the chaotic conditions of the 21st century, one who is very self-aware and, importantly, leads with precision and impact.

For far too long, many leaders have shied away from being emotionally intelligent, but the future requires the opposite. *Lead Beyond 2030* shares the skills, techniques, processes and the thinking that will dramatically impact our future."

Jane Grover
Chief Executive Officer, SMCT

"A must-read for all leaders; captivating you from the first page, it will take you on a journey of self-discovery, awareness and desire to lead from the heart with kindness, compassion and true inspiration. Infused with relevant and practical tips based on science and first-hand experience, Kennedy clearly captures the essence of what true leadership is all about and offers tools, advice and strategies to teach us how to be not only successful, but exceptional leaders. Finally, an inspiring book that gives us all hope for a wiser, more compassionate and generous leadership culture, taking us into the next decade and beyond."

Rachael Ferguson
Chief Executive Officer, SynxBody

"A must-read for executives, helping you to create lasting change in yourself, in the people you lead, and in your organisation, no matter the level of leadership position you hold. Success depends on the quality of your leadership, and *Lead Beyond 2030* is the starting point to intensifying your impact and performance. It contains multiple exercises of reflection and practical tools and techniques to unleash your most powerful self."

Amy Davidson
Regional General Manager, Westpac

"As Albert Einstein once said, 'We cannot solve our problems with the same thinking we used when we created them.' *Lead Beyond 2030* explores how business leadership is evolving; just like human development, leadership is evolving from a place of mindfulness. Being self-aware is key, and it starts with the reflection in the mirror, which needs to be nurtured with regular yet simple self-regulation. This book offers an abundance of tools, strategies and practical advice for leaders who want to reach more of their full potential."

Kathryn Zammit
Workplace Relations Advisor, Australian Hotel Association

"With broad senior executive and CEO experience across many industry sectors and an in-demand global executive coach, Caroline has a unique insight into how businesses around the world operate. This book convinces readers to cast aside conventional ideas of leadership role models, tells a story of the future of leadership and provides practical advice on how to navigate the future so you too can raise the bar high, and thrive in this fast-paced world."

Sarah Bartholomeusz
Chief Executive Officer, You Legal

"Leadership is not about talent, it's a skill, and *Lead Beyond 2030* modernises conventional leadership. It lays out the fundamental principles that give leaders the edge to expedite their career and intensify their impact. Everyone will get something out of this book, whether you're an MD leading a multimillion-dollar company, or you lead a department, a small team, or just yourself. In this age of economic uncertainty and fierce competition, there has never been a better time to adapt successfully to remain relevant."

Ken Loh
Director, Umow Lai

First published in 2020 by Hambone Publishing
Melbourne, Australia

 A catalogue record for this
book is available from the
NATIONAL
LIBRARY   National Library of Australia
OF AUSTRALIA

For information about this title, contact:
Caroline Kennedy
info@carolinekennedy.com.au
www.carolinekennedy.com.au

ISBN 978-1-922357-15-1 (paperback)
ISBN 978-1-922357-17-5 (hardback)
ISBN 978-1-922357-16-8 (ebook)

LEAD BEYOND
— 2030 —

The Nine Skills You Need to
Intensify Your Leadership Impact

CAROLINE KENNEDY
International Award-Winning CEO

TABLE OF CONTENTS

ACKNOWLEDGEMENTS

I want to thank everyone who helped me sharpen every single part of this book. This book is a result of a tremendous amount of work from a talented and committed team.

Writing a book is always harder than you think and more rewarding than you could ever imagine. It's a challenging exercise for any author, but this exercise was a challenge for my loving family too; I would disappear early in the morning before everyone was awake and lock myself away on weekends. To my husband, Peter, thank you. From giving me advice on the cover to entertaining our munchkin so I could edit, you were as crucial to the making of this book as I was. And to my son, Ethan, thank you for being my constant inspiration, buddy.

Writing a book is not the creation of a single author but rather that of a whole host of friends and associates who provide inspiration and advice. I want to thank Anne Carlin for the early editorial advice and for helping me shape the idea. Thanks also to everyone on the Hambone Publishing team who helped me so much. Special thanks to Ben, the ever-vigilant publishing manager, to Mish and Emily, my fantastic editors, and to Giovanni, the most incredible cover designer I could ever have imagined.

The people who strive to develop and lead others are the people who make this world a better place. The secret to growth is in helping others to grow. Thank you to every single leader who strives to become a better version of themselves every single day, you help others succeed. It's a heavy responsibility, to help others grow as a result of your presence and ensure that impact lasts even when you're not present.

To my clients, community, crew and all the individuals who've led me, to those I've had the privilege of leading, and to the role models I've watched lead, I want to say thank you for being the foundation and inspiration for *Lead Beyond 2030*.

To the special people who have loved and supported me for more years than I can recall—my family and friends—you always know what to say and when to say it, and you keep me sane. Thank you from the bottom of my heart.

Finally, to all those who lead courageous lives, who push past their comfort zones to get comfortable being uncomfortable, I see you, and I raise my glass to you.

My only wish for this book is that it stimulates your curiosity. Those who dare truly live life on their own terms.

MY GIFTS TO YOU

People who strive to develop and lead others are people who make this world a better place. I've learnt that helping one person might not change the world, but it can change their world (and that matters). That's why I've created these gifts.

Masterclass
This is the roadmap to increasing your executive presence, attracting more opportunities and intensifying your impact.

Test Your Leadership Scorecard
Discover your leadership score and the nine leadership accelerators to help you intensify your impact and performance.

Visit www.carolinekennedy.com.au to find them.

Download the Lead Beyond 2030 Workbook
Access the resources and exercises for all chapters in the book at www.carolinekennedy.com.au/bookresources

Get in Touch
Time, attention and energy are the most precious resources you have, so I appreciate you reading this book. Thank you for allowing

me to share it with you as you create new possibilities for yourself and those around you.

In my blog and on my social media pages, I regularly share the latest ideas and research along with my thoughts on topics such as success, high performance, influence, emotional intelligence, adaptability quotient, innovation, mindset, leadership, and human behaviour.

I'd love for you to reach out and stay connected. Until next time, you take care!

Caroline xx

f www.facebook.com/carolinekennedyau

⊙ www.instagram.com/carolinekennedyau

𝕏 www.twitter.com/ckennedyau

in www.linkedin.com/in/carolineekennedy

Introduction

It was William Shakespeare who said "All the world's a stage, And all the men and women merely players." You have the opportunity to be anyone you want. Why not be someone great? Why not be a great leader? One of my speaking coaches, Vinh, told me a story about how his father always challenged him to value the miracle of life. Vinh's story jogged a similar story and memory for me from my teenage years during a challenging time in my life. I remembered a piece of advice from a very important mentor in my life and the lesson stuck with me; actually, it changed my life.

He asked "Have you ever considered how lucky you are to be alive? In fact, how ridiculous is it that you're alive here on this earth. What would have happened if your parents never met? Would you be here? Or if we go back one generation and your grandparents didn't meet? Where would that leave you? Heck, if the Great Famine in Ireland killed your ancestors, that's your entire ancestry gone from the earth. It took millions of chance events for you to be here, so what are you going to do with this gift?"

Now, I ask you the same question - what are you going to do with your gift? The one constant in business and life is change, and I'm pretty sure an ambitious person like you doesn't want to become a dinosaur in your industry. In the past, too many leaders rested on their laurels and didn't bother with challenging the status quo – it's why we have too many old-school leaders. A new era of leadership is on the horizon, and it requires go-getters like you, to raise the bar high.

To rise to a higher level, to advance your career, to intensify your impact and performance, you need new skills, techniques and strategies to succeed in this fast-paced world.

So, let me ask you:

- **?** Are you looking for an edge to advance your career?

- **?** Do you have the right skills to lead successfully over the next decade and beyond?

- **?** Are you ready to increase your influence, your impact, your executive presence, and your ability to deliver results?

Well, *Lead Beyond 2030* is the book for you.

While some of the core elements of leadership will remain the same over time, such as creating future vision and executing strategy, our future leaders will need a new collection of skills to succeed.

In this book, you'll discover how to stay relevant and competitive with nine skill accelerators over three primary elements: leading self, leading others, and leading business. By mastering the skills outlined in this book, you'll be able to become an industry expert who delivers a consistent body of work, a compelling vision, a ground-breaking leadership style, and above all, a personal stamp that cuts across industries and decades. You'll become a key leader of influence.

Are You Comfortable with the Idea of Change?

It's the most important question of our time: how do you remain relevant in a rapidly changing world? We're on the cusp of what is arguably the most significant transformation period since the First Industrial Revolution. Businesses and leaders globally are facing a flood of disruptive influences which are predicted to spark the Fifth Industrial Revolution. The Fourth Industrial Revolution, driven by the fusion of developments in artificial intelligence (AI), robotics, and the Internet of Things (IoT), might be attempting to take humans out of industry; the fifth will seek to put them back in. The growth of AI makes your human skills more critical than ever before because they're skills that robots can't automate. We'll explore how our workplaces are evolving, the leadership skills required to thrive within a dynamic market, and how leaders and organisations can stay relevant and competitive in the next decade and beyond.

My knowledge can be your knowledge. My objective with this book is to share with you the insights I've learned over the years, most of which have come from necessity or through learning the hard way.

Who am I?

I'm an accomplished CEO in the private and corporate sector, with over 25 years leadership, mentoring, and coaching experience. I was honoured to be recognised twice by the Telstra Business Women's Awards for my achievements in business, and I was awarded the prestigious International Stevie Award in New York in November 2019.

As an experienced CEO, I've led multinational companies with annual revenues up to $250 million, and managed over 500 staff via ten direct reports. I've delivered outcomes such as taking a company from $38 million to $50 million in 18 months during the global financial crisis. My forte is creating high-performing teams and delivering results. I have a natural talent for seeing patterns and insights that others don't, to propel both leadership and business performance.

The career I built has taken me from restaurant manager at Ayers Rock Resort, to business manager of Hamilton Island Weddings, to expat resort management in Thailand. Returning to Australia, I held director-level positions at resort properties in Broome and Port Douglas. I was appointed CEO of one of Australia's largest wholesale travel companies, and became a pioneer, as the first female CEO to lead a network of builders and Australia's largest building franchise group. My career has spanned roles in diverse industries and the journey has been far from a straight line.

As an award-winning executive coach, I draw on my extensive background in business and leadership, bringing a multi-dimensional approach which combines coaching, mentoring, and consulting methodology to break comfort zones and facilitate long-term growth and development. My methods of coaching are neuroscience-based to achieve rapid high performance.

I've worked with many individuals and organisations hungry to reach their full potential: executive management, managing directors, CEOs, directors in the education space, IT owners, medical executives, engineering directors, Deloitte, PwC, Wesfarmers, and more.

I've spent the last three years researching and interviewing hundreds of experts and leaders, and *Lead Beyond 2030* is based on this pool of qualitative and quantitative research. The resulting conclusion was clear: we will need a new type of leader to guide teams and organisations through the next decade and beyond. I'll share examples with you, and all names and references will be changed to protect people's identity.

Leaders of 2030: identify, nurture, and empower. This book shares the megatrend related to the skills required to lead yourself, your team, and your organisation into the future. You'll learn how to master three fundamental skills, which will be powerful differentiators in the demanding twenty-first century.

The individual skills are:

Leading Self
Emotional intelligence
Self-awareness
Building authority
Executive presence

Leading Others
Leveraging human behaviour
Influence
Persuasion to empower high performance

Leading Business
Adaptability and innovation
Critical thinking
Creative problem-solving

The rapidly changing landscape influences the need for business leaders to adapt the skills at their disposal if they're to remain competitive and take advantage of opportunities. If you want to stay relevant and competitive and to grow and thrive in the future, you need to invest in a way to develop these skills further to intensify your impact and performance. They will all need to be applied as we move towards our new future.

This book will help you propel your career, as you invest in yourself and the skills of your team. The ability to swiftly develop new skills has never been more critical to keep up with the pace of change in the market.

Many leaders and organisations have an endless supply of technical knowledge and years of experience. Still, they continue to struggle because they lack emotional intelligence, which is the foundation of self-leadership. When you excel at self-leadership, you excel at leading others, placing you ahead of the game. You become a game-changing world-class leader who is paving the way.

What Do We Explore?

This book is divided into three parts: *Leading Self, Leading Others,* and *Leading Business.* In part one, Leading Self, we thoroughly assess how emotional intelligence skills are essential in nearly every area of workplace performance.

Also in part one, we'll take a closer look at authority and executive presence, and how you can further enhance yours. Authority and presence are the factors which distinguish a thought leader from the pack. People with presence look confident, calm, and composed. When they speak, people listen, and when they leave, the party is over. Presence is about your ability to inspire confidence, commitment, and trust. It inspires people to pay attention and follow you. It opens doors and helps develop connections critical to your career goals.

Part two, Leading Others, examines influence and persuasion. We will conduct an in-depth analysis of how to enhance and adapt your leadership and communication styles to align your people with change and high performance. We'll discover how to communicate in ways that get people to think and act differently and, importantly, to take action. Influential leaders foster skills which enable them to lead teams and organisations faster and influence others outside of their sphere of responsibility.

Humans fall into habitual ways of thinking without realising, so it's necessary for us to learn more about human behaviour. The techniques outlined in this book are designed to help you support others in seeing how their default mindset is not serving them well. That's where great leaders can help people to tap into their talent and discover their capabilities. You're only as good at the people around you. Let's discover how you can create an 'A' team of high performers who are kicking goals every single day, using their initiative, coming up with big ideas and solutions, and delivering above and beyond expectation.

In the third section, Leading Business, we'll look towards the future, and establish the critical skills required to thrive in this brave new world. The Future of Jobs report (2018), released by The World Economic Forum, outlined the essential skills the future demands of us—active problem solving, critical thinking, and adaptability—all of which require cognitive flexibility from leaders. This final section will show you how to sharpen these skills to become a better leader.

The foundations for my career success are keeping up with change both in myself and in business; developing my skills continually;

implementing foresight; never accepting the status quo; and always wanting to be a better version of myself to serve others.

I've witnessed how industries and leaders have failed to adapt to shifting market conditions and changing key stakeholder trends in real-time. They became no longer relevant, and I wasn't going to allow this to happen to me or to businesses I worked with. Lead Beyond 2030 was born out of my desire for growth and it shares the skills that I teach to the CEOs, executives, and senior leaders I work with now.

Imagine for a moment that you stick with what you are doing. Things look bad; your career isn't growing, you're not having an impact, your performance is not at the top of your game, you're not seen as a leader with influence or executive presence, you do not realise your full potential...

If you get this right, here's what happens: people line up to work with you, you attract opportunities, and you earn more money. You've intensified your impact and created a personal stamp that cuts across industries and decades. Let me share with you my wealth of expertise and teach you to become a leader for the future.

PART I

LEADING SELF

———

CHAPTER ONE

Embrace Emotional Intelligence as Your New Superpower

Emotional Intelligence (EQ) is the skill and capacity to be in sync with yourself, your emotions, and the emotions of those around you. With EQ, you'll become the leader everyone wants to work for. With EQ comes a sense of situational awareness so powerful that when you master it, you'll be the envy of many.

Psychologists Peter Salovey and John Mayer first classified and developed the EQ theory in 1990. They defined EQ as, "The ability to monitor one's own and other's emotions, to discriminate among them, and to use the information to guide one's thinking and actions".

Daniel Goleman, another psychologist, helped popularise the theory of emotional intelligence, and he defines it as, "The ability to manage feelings so that they are expressed appropriately and effectively, enabling people to work together smoothly toward their common goal".

Leaders who lack EQ don't effectively evaluate the needs, wants, and expectations of the people they lead. It's that simple. Great leaders are self-aware and understand that how they communicate can impact their team. They can also read and assess others through their verbal and non-verbal communication.

In his work, Daniel Goleman fragmented emotional intelligence into personal skills and social skills. Under these two segments fall a variety of skills which are the components of emotional intelligence. Before we go into depth about these components, let's take a look at EQ at a high level.

1 - Identify Emotions

The most basic skill in EQ is recognising your emotions. You can respond appropriately to situations when you have an accurate read on what is going on, and you can influence like a pro. When you misread emotional data, it can be awkward and virtually impossible to recover from. Reading your own feelings and emotions and those of the people around you is critical to building a workplace that thrives, one that everyone wants to be part of. It can be very difficult to work with someone who's checked-out or doesn't care, never noticing how you are or asking about you. This type of person can seem removed and not human at all.

Emotions, moods and temperaments are not created equal. Let me explain; emotions can be short lived and generally last for only a few minutes or in extreme cases for a more extended period. These feeling are positive or negative and can feel slight or intense, and are usually triggered by a specific person or situation.

Moods are your emotional state, part of your emotional rhythm, but less intense than an emotion, typically moods last for hours, but they can last for days or longer sometimes. You've heard people say they got up on the wrong side of the bed, this is usually people waking up feeling a bit off, and it can last all day. Moods get triggered by events, such as learning about a betrayal. You can also fall into a mood for no specific reason.

Temperament is associated with your character type or the personality, you're born with, or you acquire it from a young age, it's also based on your beliefs and values. A lack of self awareness around your temperament can lead to blind spots.

2 – Use Emotions (to Aid Thinking)

Your brain interprets what's going on around you from your thoughts, beliefs, and memories. How you interpret events influences how you think and behave. Positive emotions can result in positive thoughts, which can result in positive decisions and therefore, positive behaviour. For example, you achieve a significant result; you're happy about the outcome, you'll behave in a confident manner, which leads to assertive decision making. This is a cycle where good thoughts lead to good behaviour which leads to a good mood and so on.

Getting into the right mindset enables you to lead the way. Use your feelings to enhance your thinking. By doing this you can channel better reasoning, problem solving, decision making, and creative thinking. Of course, on the flip side, your cognitive system can be disrupted by negative emotions such as fear and anxiety.

Research cited in *The negativity bias* shows that people with a negative or sad mindset often search for problems and fixate on unnecessary details, it's called negativity bias. Those with a more positive mindset are better at generating new ideas and solutions to problems. I worked with a boss once who was unable to look at a problem and find a solution; all he wanted to do was fixate on the problem and blame other people for it. We could not move past the problem and it was frustrating. There was never a nice word that came out of his mouth about people. These combined attributes created a culture of blame and resentment. It was one of the worst cultures I've worked in. It showed me what not to do as a leader. As a result of poor leadership, the business was stale and was unable to innovate, grow, or make any progress, whilst competitors thrived.

3 – Recognise and Comprehend Emotions

Emotions are a fundamental part of your consciousness so it's important to understand them. Think of emotions as simple and complex terms that provide you with a better understanding of their effect in shaping human behaviour. For example, combined emotions such as disgust and anger form contempt. You can use this understanding to master influencing others.

Consider the progress of emotions too (irritation to frustration to anger), and how they transition. The influencing skill involves the capacity to analyse emotions and their causes, along with the ability to predict how people may feel and react in different situations.

For example, anger is a high-level term sitting at the top of the iceberg, but if we look below the surface we can identify various feelings and how they manifest, as illustrated.

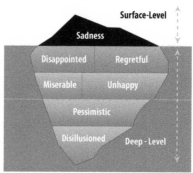

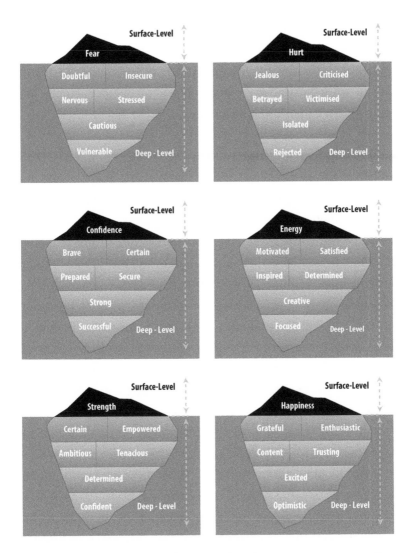

Emotions are consistent but emotional temperaments vary from person to person. Those who have negative emotional systems are easily triggered, have powerful reactions, and are tougher to reason with and influence.

Mastering your ability to influence involves considering emotional temperaments. For example, what would happen if

I said to a frustrated colleague, "You need to calm down?" How would he then feel? This ability is not isolated to colleagues; it's applicable with anyone you encounter, including family, friends, and co-workers. Understanding emotional temperaments helps you to master the skill of influence.

4 - Manage Emotions

The fourth component of EQ is about the ability to regulate your own moods and emotions and to recognise emotions in other people. When you're managing your feelings, you're able to monitor, differentiate, and label them accurately. When you're able to modify these feelings, you remain in control. Poor decision-making can be a result of ignoring your feelings or intuitions. Keep an open mind, tap into your feelings, and learn from them. Conversely, there will be times when it's better to disengage with an emotion and address it at a later point, so as to avoid blowing a fuse at the wrong moment.

Anger is one the most misunderstood emotions. It's not necessarily a bad feeling. In fact, when used appropriately to overcome injustice, adversity, or bias, anger can be a useful tool. Anger can arise when we feel frustrated, cheated, or taken advantage of. It can be blindsiding, especially if we don't deal with it, and it can cause us to act in negative or belligerent ways. I experienced a situation recently where miscommunication led to mind reading: people thought they knew what the others involved were thinking, and began creating thoughts around situations that weren't real. This caused one person to feel frustrated. She became angry to the point where she would not see reason, and so she withdrew and acted in an unsociable way. This person was struggling to use her EQ skills and chose not to manage her emotions. I'm sure you can remember similar situations you've experienced, too.

5 - Emotional Intelligence – Not Always What You Think

EQ is partially about controlling your feelings and emotions, but mainly it's about how you use and develop them. Emotional Intelligence is not about your skills and aptitudes, nor your cognitive intelligence (IQ), both of which we'll cover shortly. It's not how you are perceived or what you have achieved; it's how you read others around you and are aware of their feelings as well as your own. It's about maintaining an emotional awareness and sensitivity, developing the skills to help you to stay ahead of the game so you can become the leader everyone respects and follows. Because you understand yourself and others, you can lead the way.

The Four Pillars of Emotional Intelligence

Goleman's model shows four areas of emotional intelligence: **self-awareness, self-management, social awareness**, and **relationship management**. All are important in mastering emotional intelligence, so let's explore each one.

Self-awareness

The best leaders are self-aware, and it's been found to be one of the most important skills for leaders to develop. A study by Korn Ferry, which looked at the performance of 486 publicly listed companies, found that when organisations have employees with a higher level of self-awareness, they have stronger performance. Yet with so much of the old-school management style still in action at the C-suite level, self-awareness seems to be in short supply among leaders.

A study by Hay Group found that executive women display more self-awareness than their male counterparts. The study of 17,000 people from across the world established that 19 per cent of women executives interviewed showed self-awareness, compared to 4 per cent of their male counterparts.

Regardless of gender, the overall percentages confirm there is plenty of opportunity for growth here. The World Economic Forum future of jobs report also cited EQ as one of the top skills referred to as a non-negotiable for leaders in the 21st Century and beyond, so now is the time to embrace it, or get left behind. Self-awareness is the starting place to develop your leadership skills further.

Self-awareness is important in leadership as well as in your daily life because it supplies you with a comprehensive grasp of who you are as a person and leader, and how you connect and show up in the world. It's about knowing what you're good at while recognising that you have more to learn. When you're self-aware, you know both your strengths and weaknesses, and you recognise how to manage them in the workplace and beyond.

To improve your self-awareness, consider incorporating reflection time into your day. For example, you could think about how people reacted to you and how connected you were while working with and managing others.

Be honest in your reflection to capitalise on self-awareness. You won't get anywhere if you bury your head in the sand. It's also beneficial to seek out feedback from those you trust, and people who'll be honest with you and whose feedback you value.

For a more formal approach you can access feedback through a 360 assessment. In a 360, both your peers and your managers provide anonymous feedback on all aspects of your behaviour.

Another method which I've used to develop my self-awareness is to seek out regular feedback from my team. For this to be effective, however, you must be able to let go of ego, learn to ask good questions, and listen without feeling the need to justify or defend your actions.

In my coaching work with executives, I've had a front row seat to the immense power that is leadership self-awareness. When leaders are challenged, their response is usually an attempt to justify or defend their actions. I call this out when it occurs because it holds people back. What's interesting is that after a few sessions of calling it out, most executives become increasingly self-aware, and this is where the magic happens. This is where real change occurs because the starting point for growth is awareness. Without it, you will never grow.

Self-management

The second core component of emotional intelligence is self-management. Self-management is the ability to control your own reactions and impulses. It includes emotional self-control, transparency, adaptability, initiative, and optimism.

Have you ever been so frustrated at work that you've wanted to walk out in the middle of your workday? I remember an incident where one of my peers was struggling to understand my point of view because he was not self-aware and couldn't view any other perspective besides his own. At the end of a meeting one day, we were holding a discussion in which he was being one dimensional, unable to see from any other point of view. In frustration, I picked up my laptop, slammed it shut, stood up, and walked out of the meeting. When I look back now, I can see that I was unable to manage my emotions. Luckily for me, I soon developed these vital skills (otherwise, my career wouldn't have gone far). We are all human and we all make mistakes, but positive change begins with the awareness of our weaknesses. If the negative behaviour continues, there is a lack of progress and you'll be the leader no one wants to work with.

Other self-management skills include self-confidence, patience, resilience, persistence, emotional regulation, and perceptiveness. These skills support you in working towards your goals, developing high performance at work, and making your work environment the place people want to be.

One of the most critical skills for self-management is self-confidence. To work for a leader who is constantly changing their mind or second-guessing themself is to work in the frustrating chaos of confusion and indecision. Self-confidence means trusting your judgement and instinct. It doesn't mean that you're overconfident in the decisions you make. Making decisions is difficult, but trust your instincts to guide you in the right direction. Use the information available to support your decision making. Everyone can make decisions. Anyone can develop strong decision-making skills using simple techniques, which we'll explore in more detail in the chapters on problem solving and critical thinking.

Self-confidence is most important when it comes to problem solving and difficult tasks. For example, let's say you've been asked to make a decision that impacts your entire team, such as needing to restructure your department to reduce costs. Now, such a task most likely requires redundancies or cutting back hours, but as a self-confident individual who operates with a high degree of EQ, you won't become overwhelmed and stressed out. You know all you can do is carefully evaluate the options before making the best decision. Of course, your empathy will help you when evaluating the options, but you'll do what needs to be done. You can rest well knowing that you've done all you can to support your people.

Self-confidence also fuels others' confidence in you. If your boss knows that you're sure of yourself and you operate with a high level of EQ, then she is more likely to trust you with the assigned task. Your colleagues will also feel like they can turn to you when a crisis arises. This trust is a great asset.

Social Awareness

If we continue to follow Goleman's model, we find three key components of social awareness. They are:

1. **Empathy** – being considerate of other people's needs, concerns, perspectives, and emotions. Stepping into their shoes even for a moment.

2. **Organisational awareness** – understanding the politics within an organisation and how they impact people.

3. **Customer-centric** – the ability to consider and meet the needs, concerns, perspectives, and emotions of customers or clients.

When you're aware of social situations it means you take into consideration what people want and how they think. You then plan how you'll communicate with them to meet that need. This is different to manipulation. It's what I call influence because it's done with the genuine intent to support and help others. This book includes a whole chapter on the topic of influence as it is by far one of the most important aspects of EQ.

Empathy (not to be confused with sympathy) is the ability to listen to others and to put yourself in their shoes and understand how they are feeling. You don't need to agree with them, but you're able to see their perspective and to consider the situation from their point of view. This helps to improve communication and trust.

Organisational awareness at its core is the ability to read key influential relationships, understand organisational dynamics, influence others and handle the demands of leadership. It's about leveraging the forces at work in the organisation, alongside clear, established values. Individuals skilled in this area capitalise on the structure and relationships that make the organisation run and know who to influence to gain the desired outcome.

Customer-centric means putting the customer at the heart of everything that you do, so you can achieve goals that are aligned with overall organisational objectives. In the Leading Business section of this book, we discover the importance of adaptability, innovation, problem solving and critical thinking in ensuring future relevance. Remaining relevant all starts with putting the customer at the heart of everything that you do, considering the customer's emotional buy habits, changing needs, and perspectives, and adapting to those needs so you don't end up an irrelevant brand to consumers like Blackberry or Kodak.

Alongside empathy, we have nurturing relationships. Nurturing relationships is the demonstration of genuine care, as opposed to the courtesy often demonstrated out of obligation. We can show genuine appreciation for people's efforts with our words and actions. In setting a collaborative tone with others, no matter the situation, you are keeping their best interests front of mind—without losing focus on the creation of win-win outcomes in line with your goals.

Research by Sara Konrath, a University of Michigan researcher shows that our levels of empathy are lower today than they were 30 years ago. Social isolation is one theory, and the main culprit. Research blames the use of digital communiqué such as video conferencing and social media for the reduction in empathy, but we've allowed it to happen, so really we're to blame. Where there is no empathy, there is no trust. If I don't know what you're thinking and feeling, I'm not going to trust you. Since trust is essential for successful leadership, this lack of empathy has huge implications. It doesn't need to be this way and the future demands that we up our game.

Relationship Management

The last piece of the puzzle is relationship management, which involves developing others, inspirational leadership, influence, being a catalyst, conflict management, collaboration, and teamwork. We'll cover more of this later too.

Relationship management is the aspect of your EQ that allows you to be successful in empowering and inspiring others, helping them to become the best versions of themselves so they can reach their full potential. It's about how you set other people up for success. It is also vital in conflict resolution, having difficult conversations, leading others through change, and empowering others in the direction of a shared goal.

The key skills of relationship management are:

- **Communication** – planning your communications in advance to ensure you use the correct emotional tone and understand and consider people's triggers.

- **Developing others** – setting people up for success by identifying their strengths and offering help for development, including challenging them to step out of their comfort zones in order to grow.

- **Building elite performance/teamwork and collaboration** – defining a criterion of success, allowing everyone to contribute to the overall objectives and goals. Setting clear expectations and KPIs for individual accountability.

- **Mastering influence** – focusing on tapping into and understanding what's important to others by having the ability to build alignment and win support.

- **Inspirational leadership** – it's not about the title, it's about leading effectively so others choose to follow. Leaders create other leaders and are able to be led.

- **Being the catalyst** – be prepared to question traditional ideals, think critically, initiate new ideas, and challenge others' thinking and problem solving, recognising when change is needed and creating a culture of adaptability.

- **Managing conflict** – understanding when situations are escalating towards conflict and take decisive action to resolve issues. Tackling difficult conversations head on as opposed to retreating from them.

- **Building connections** – cultivating a symbiotic network of friends, colleagues and acquaintances.

Example – Jeff Bezos

There are many leaders who have mastered emotional intelligence. Amazon's Jeff Bezos is a good example. A few years ago, he was criticised by The New York Times, when

Jodi Kantor and David Streitfeld wrote an article targeting Amazon for its harsh working environment and demanding employment standards. Many Amazon supervisors recall, "Preparing for meetings was like getting ready for a court case, and they'd try to avoid losing members of their teams, by coming armed with supporting evidence and paper trails to defend those accused. Or they'd adopt a strategy of choosing a person to sacrifice to protect their crucial players", reported the New York Times.

It wasn't the only criticism of Amazon's leadership. Journalist and author of The Everything Store: Jeff Bezos and the Age of Amazon, Brad Stone writes, "Amazon's performance review method is a reproduction of Amazon CEO Jeff Bezos' demanding standards ... Jeff appears to expect his executives to raise the stakes in terms of performance with every promotion and new recruitment. He believes that only the top talent should advance within the organisation."

Bezos took swift action by addressing the claims that were raised and turned the situation into an opportunity for personal leadership growth by announcing changes within the company and policies. Amazon announced, "We're introducing a new simplified annual review process that focuses on our employees' strengths, not the absenteeism or weaknesses. We learn from our employees and we'll continue to build on the program based on our employees' feedback."

Bezos could have become defensive and fought the claims, but instead, he used his awareness skills to reflect on what the employees and public wanted. A prime example of emotional intelligence in action.

By examining the strategic approach to this situation, you'll see how to differentiate between emotion and the need to take action. First, Bezos promoted action in response to the honest feedback of others. The feedback was constant, suggesting a pattern and truth. Second, he inhibited action in response to anger and hostility. Bezos would have felt attacked, which may have prompted anger and a sense of hostility. However, he used his instinct and awareness to guide his decision making and response to this situation. Could this be the essence of wisdom?

Impact Your Career and Role

By now, you've started to consider the impact your emotional intelligence can have on your career, your leadership, and your role. Any weaknesses in EQ can hinder your job, and if you're a leader it can impair your performance.

A TalentSmart EQ study of over a million individuals concluded that middle managers stand out with the highest EQ workplace scores. EQ scores drop off a cliff for director titles and above, with CEOs roles having the lowest results. Interestingly, although this study shows that in the workplace CEOs have the lowest EQ scores, it noted that the top-performing CEOs are the ones with a high level of emotional intelligence. It doesn't mean executives with low EQs don't get promoted, in fact all too often they do, but they don't outperform their high-EQ competitors.

Organisations that select leaders who don't have well-rounded skills are selling themselves short in terms of performance levels. Research carried out by The Carnegie Institute of Technology concluded that our human skills, such as our ability to lead others, negotiate, and communicate, equate to 85 per cent of our financial success.

Poor interpersonal skills, difficulty in handling change, and not being a good leader or team player were the three leading causes of career and leadership failure. According to many research papers, key predictors of success include your ability to:

- ❏ Control your emotions

- ❏ Manage frustrations

- ❏ Handle issues, problem solve and find solutions

- ❏ Manage your social interactions with others

- ❏ Influence others

Do you know any socially inept, highly intelligent people? Or introverts who are socially awkward? Maybe it's you, and that's okay! I'm an introvert who is socially awkward, but I've taught myself how to show up with the charisma and swagger needed to be a visionary leader, and you can too.

I'd like you to think about a leader or manager who you believe to be successful. What qualities or skills do they have that contribute to their success?

1. ....

2. ....

3. ....

4. ....

5. ....

If you have high levels of emotional intelligence, good intellectual abilities, and good technical skills, you're well placed for future career success.

CHAPTER TWO

Emotionally Intelligent Leadership is the Future

We hear stories of highly skilled, intelligent executives stepping into leadership positions only to fail miserably. One of my favourite examples is of Martin Winterkorn, the former CEO of Volkswagen. He ran the company during a disastrous scandal which saw company engineers install software that manipulated emissions in over ten million diesel vehicles.

What is to be noted here is not just the mistake, but the way it was handled by the executive. It is reported that Winterkorn asserted ignorance of any wrongdoing, essentially not taking responsibility for his actions. Meanwhile, Volkswagen reports that they handed a warning of potential misconduct to Winterkorn. He is a prime example of what not to do, having displayed such a lack of emotional intelligence. He believed he shouldn't make any mistakes or be seen to have made a mistake at all.

This isn't a problem unique to executives; leaders at all levels can spin important issues with their bosses or colleagues for fear of appearing incompetent. These are examples of where ego limits leadership excellence.

On the other hand, I could tell you stories about people without overly remarkable technical abilities who soared when stepping into a leadership role. Under some circumstances, ordinary people communicate more effectively and cope better than highly educated, academically intelligent people generally might. Initially, I thought I was never going to be able to see the top of the corporate ladder without the "necessary" education; I soon learnt that there are more important aspects to becoming a leader than scholarship.

Despite the odds, I did manage to climb to the top, and went on to lead multimillion-dollar organisations, only studying an MBA later in my career. During this time, I came to understand that the most effective leaders have one common characteristic critical to their success—a high degree of emotional intelligence (EQ).

I'm not saying that intellect and technical skills are inessential; they matter, but mainly as entry-level requirements for roles. My research when working with hundreds of leaders, along with many other recent studies, such as Dulewicz (2020) and Sistad (2020) categorically shows that emotional intelligence is absolutely necessary for leadership excellence. Without it, a person can have all the smarts in the world, and still won't make a great leader. Today, this skill set is lacking in many leaders, particularly the old-school leaders who believe in leading with an iron fist.

I bet you're wondering the impact of EQ is on your career and professional success. Research suggests a lot! Dr Travis Bradberry, author of Emotional Intelligence 2.0, tested EQ together with 33 additional vital workplace skills, and the study found it to be the strongest indicator of performance, linked with 58 per cent of job success.

The research also tells us that individuals with lower levels of EQ take home an average of $29,000 less per annum than those with higher degrees of EQ. At the top C-suite level this gap is even wider. I know one thing for sure: no one in their right mind wants to be on the low end of their earning potential!

Spotting the Signs of Low Emotional Intelligence

To combat a lack of emotional intelligence, you must first be able to identify it. Let's discuss some of the common things I hear from those working with leaders who lack emotional intelligence.

I've heard so many stories....

"I went to a professional development event where I created a new innovated program, and when I got back, instead of being pleased for me, my manager said 'Don't forget, we own anything you create.' So, I stopped trying to improve things. Not because I didn't want the business to have them, but because my manager seemed so greedy and controlling."

> "We used to laugh about one of the managers who always complained about not being able to get or keep staff. He couldn't understand why. Nobody wanted to work for him because he was so inflexible and a stickler for the rules. It was a punishment to be sent to work there."

> "I tried to explain what was going on in the team, and I could see the leader's eyes were open, but her ears were closed. There was nothing I could do."

I've seen the damage done by leaders with little emotional intelligence many times in my work as a CEO, leading multinational organisations, and now mentoring and coaching executives.

What Are the Signs of Low Emotional Intelligence?

Lacking Empathy

Without empathy, it's difficult to see things from a different perspective. As a leader, this means you can't relate to your team members or understand their emotions.

For example, a team leader introduces a new system which their team is upset about. The leader doesn't understand why because everything he said is logical and straightforward. He thought he'd explained it well and can't understand why his team might be concerned or fearful. This indicates that the leader lacks empathy.

Unempathetic leaders struggle to handle tough conversations and conflicts. They find it difficult to read signs and signals for help and can alienate their colleagues and team members because they perceive their own perspective to be every person's reality. Humans are neurologically wired for empathy, and in leadership, empathy alone won't cut the mustard; the magic happens when you incorporate tough empathy, which we discuss later.

Blaming Others

One of the biggest signs of a lack of emotional intelligence is blame-shifting. This may present itself as a leader stating that they gave their team all the information to get it right, so why didn't they? The truth is that it's not always information that is needed; sometimes people need support and guidance.

Thinking Others Are Too Sensitive

A person lacking emotional intelligence may be confused when confronted with a negative response to something which seems clear and straightforward from their perspective. They don't recognise that when a person disagrees or feels strongly about what has been said, it doesn't mean they are overly sensitive or emotional.

Reacting to Emotions

Those lacking emotional intelligence often act on their raw emotions and this can lead to outbursts or strong reactions. No matter how frustrated we become or how upset we are, as leaders it is not wise to react in this way.

Combatting Low Emotional Intelligence

Here are some tell-tale signs that you might need to focus on improving your emotional intelligence:

- ❏ You have high expectations of yourself and others.

- ❏ You get frustrated and impatient when people don't get to the point quickly enough.

- ❏ When people react sensitively to your comments, you assume they're overreacting.

- ❏ You jump right in with your claims and rigorously defend them.

- ❏ You tend to find others at fault for issues that arise.

- ❏ Others tend to expect you to know how they feel, and you find this annoying.

- ❏ You tend to avoid conversations by changing the subject.

If you can recognise yourself in some of these signs, you may need to improve your EQ. But don't panic! You can learn to develop and polish the skills that are crucial in your ability to work with others. I am a prime example of the fact that emotional intelligence can be learnt. When I began my career over 25 years ago, I had little EQ, but working on it changed my career for the better.

You can develop your emotional intelligence, you can rewire your responses to feelings, you can change how you think and react, and you can alter your behaviour. You can improve your emotional intelligence. However, it won't happen overnight. Enhancing and sustaining emotional intelligence takes an intensive effort over several months and maybe even years. So, why would you want to improve your emotional intelligence skills? Well, the benefits involve mental clarity, higher productivity, higher performance, magnetising talents, inspiring people, reduced stress, and reduced anxiety, to name a few.

Leaders with high emotional intelligence skills are sought after because they make the best bosses and leaders. People love to work for the best (think Steve Jobs, Richard Branson, Elon Musk and Jacinda Ardern). They're like magnets for talented people. It's human nature to seek out people who bring out the best in us: leaders who challenge us to perform at an elite level. Individuals who work for leaders with high EQ are more creative, more dedicated, more resilient, and most likely to deliver desirable outcomes.

When you develop your emotional intelligence skills, you show up as your authentic self. You're able to empower and inspire people to achieve their goals and objectives. Your courage, passion, visionary thinking, and powerful persuasive skills will be evident to those around you.

Take some time to think about which of the EQ skills would help you the most, and what improvement you could create if you master these skills.

Compassion in Action – Jacinda Ardern

Let's take a closer look at emotional intelligence and leadership in action. After the horrific attacks in New Zealand in March 2019, everyone was watching Jacinda Ardern, most of us with astonishment and respect. She showed us what real leadership looks like, in the moment. Jacinda Ardern is a role model who leads with compassion, kindness, empathy, and love alongside strength, determination, and bravery. Being able to show these emotions publicly was an act of emotional intelligence because they are connection skills. They weren't used for attention or manipulation, but to genuinely connect with those she was leading.

Her leadership made us stop and pay attention. In Australia and around the world we've long suffered under weak or half-hearted leadership which has one eye on the voting public or the next promotion. We've longed for a leader who cares about us and listens to what we say. We've ached for real leadership but forgotten what it looks like. Jacinda Ardern has shown us what we've been missing and, more importantly, proved that it still exists and is human.

Leadership is an industry. The role of the leader has been pulled apart, picked over, and reshaped into some unachievable model of superiority and prestige. We've made leadership something bigger than us. We've made it about power and success, and we've shaped it into something we think demands respect simply because of the title. We've turned it into a label instead of a way of life. We strive to become leaders by entitlement instead of leading through our actions.

Jacinda Ardern has shattered that perception with her dignified, compassionate, influential leadership. Her actions weren't driven by politics. She wasn't choosing her behaviour based on stereotypes, nor building a platform for self-promotion. She wasn't worrying about gender models of leadership. She just got out there and did her job. She led her country. She was a human being trying to care for her people and guide them through a tragic time.

Making new laws might help control the way society operates, but it won't heal the emotional wounds of a country. Sometimes the best thing you can do as a leader, one who acts with emotional intelligence, is to pull your people together. That's where Jacinda Ardern stood out. She was completely genuine in her empathy, integrity, and her actions. We watched her grieve, hug the families of the victims, and defy terror. We watched her pull her people together and unite them as one nation standing together.

If there is one good thing to come out of this tragedy, it's the shining light of genuinely human leadership. It's strong, decisive, kind, and compassionate. It's responsive and it's real, with no other motive than to heal and protect. It's unapologetically human and vulnerable and emotional.

We can all learn from Jacinda Ardern. She reminded us what a leader is, and it's not a title. You can step up as a leader whenever you choose to and do it by tapping into your emotional intelligence. Our natural human qualities have been overlooked and underrated for too long, for without them, leadership is purely technical.

Society is demanding natural leaders; we've underestimated the impact of emotional intelligence and how it intensifies a leader's influence. Jacinda Ardern can't change the world on her own. She needs us to follow her example. Can you step up? Can you become a better version of yourself and be a strong, emotionally intelligent leader?

Self-Directed Change

There are several models for improving your emotional intelligence. One example is the model for self-directed change. Self-directed change involves identifying what you'd like to learn or change, and taking full ownership of your knowledge and development. For example, you determine that you'd like to improve your EQ skills, but you might already have some well-developed skills within that bracket, and others that need strengthening. You can work with a coach or mentor to decide the skills to focus on and create a timeline for developing them.

This model encourages the understanding of the gap between the current state and the ideal state. It prompts questions such as:

? What are my aspirations and goals?

? Is my understanding of my strengths and areas of development accurate?

? Do I see myself as others see me? This question is subjective on many levels, therefore, I encourage you to learn how others see you and why. Until you understand what others say about you, you cannot internalise this information.

If you feel you need to change and to improve as a leader, consider trying to accept these statements as truths:

❒ I am responsible for my feelings.

❒ I am accountable and take ownership for my behaviour and attitude.

- ☐ I can choose how I respond to people, situations, and issues.

- ☐ No one can make me upset, angry, happy, etc.

- ☐ Identifying my options empowers me to reflect upon my behaviour.

- ☐ Becoming self-aware is an excellent way to improve my responses and behaviour.

- ☐ I can learn and practise new and more effective responses.

- ☐ I can empower people and inspire commitment and action.

- ☐ My actions must focus on the good of others over self-interest.

- ☐ I maintain a high level of integrity, clearly communicate, and lead by example.

- ☐ The performance of my team starts and ends with me.

Emotional intelligence is a skill like any other, and if you don't have this skill naturally, this book will provide a solid foundation on which you can develop it. Here are a few strategies you can commence right now:

- **Assess yourself.** Take some time out to look at what makes you, YOU. What do you like about yourself? What do you dislike? Dig deep to find what drives you and what your moral compass tells you about the choices you make.

- **Get feedback.** Talk to your coach or people you know well and trust. Ask them to describe you as they see you. Remember to listen for the not-so-good aspects and not just the good.

- **Work on your strengths.** Consciously practice what you're good at. This is an area where you already excel, so use it.

- **Work on your weaknesses.** Get some help to develop new skills and practice them regularly. If you don't know where to start, choose a skill that you know is especially important in your current role. Think back over your mistakes and the tough times you've been through. What might have helped you get a better result for you and your team?

- **Reflect.** You'll find this suggestion coming up regularly in this book. Self-reflection is a good way to learn from your experiences and assess how you handled things. You need to be honest with yourself and accept that you won't always be at your best. That's perfectly normal. EQ grows when you accept that about yourself and the people you're with.

To summarise:

- ❑ Assess your skills and conduct an inventory of the skills you need to develop.

- ❑ When you've identified the skills you want to develop, prioritise and focus on a few.

- [ ] All skills require daily practice until you become unconsciously competent.

- [ ] When dealing with specific situations, consider the environment and pinpoint the skills required.

- [ ] Observe and reflect on how to improve constantly.

- [ ] Expecting immediate results is unrealistic.

- [ ] Use mistakes as opportunities to learn.

In the upcoming chapters, we deep dive into improving your emotional intelligence.

CHAPTER THREE

———

Measuring EQ – It's About More Than Tools

EQ matters at work. We know there's a strong relationship between emotional intelligence and work performance. Leaders with high EQ create happier teams which are motivated, engaged, empowered, and creative. Those with low EQ lead unhappy teams which are disengaged, unresponsive, and prone to bullying, criticising and blaming each other.

As global competition grows and pressures increase on business to adapt or to get ahead of the game, we need to pay closer attention to the impact of emotion on the people we work with. Emotional intelligence is the new currency every company is looking for — particularly at leadership level.

Can We Measure Emotional Intelligence in the Workplace?

How can the EQ of leaders and teams be assessed? How can we see where more EQ is needed to help shift the company to the forefront of industry?

Can EQ be measured? The answer is yes, and there are many tools you can use to do so. The three main methods are by self-assessment, feedback from others, and performance measures.

Self-assessment

You already know that it's possible to take stock of your interpersonal skills through self-assessment to get a glimpse into your own level of EQ.

Self-assessment only works when we are honest with ourselves and that's harder than we realise. People can be afraid of what they'll find out about themselves so it's not unusual to fudge a figure here and there. They probably feel as though that's a survival technique but, in the end, it's a big mistake.

Another problem with self-assessment is that some of us overestimate our abilities while others underrate themselves. The results are coloured by our level of confidence and our willingness to be honest.

Regardless of these flaws, self-assessment is a challenging tool which can open our eyes to a new view of ourselves. It's worth doing.

Leadership Test – Nine Accelerators

Are you willing to try self-assessment? Jump over to my website at *carolinekennedy.com.au* and take the free leadership test to discover how well you score against the nine leadership accelerators. Once complete, you'll receive a seventeen-page report which provides suggestions on how to improve your score for each of the accelerators so you can intensify your impact and performance.

The Emotional Quotient Inventory 2.0 (EQ-i-2.0)

This is a popular tool. It's a self-assessment which can be completed online in 30 minutes. Based on Bar-On's model of emotional-social intelligence, it covers 15 competencies across the areas of self-perception, self-expression, Interpersonal skills, decision making, and stress management.

Multidimensional Emotional Intelligence Assessment-Workplace (MEIA-W)

The MEIA-W was designed to measure emotional intelligence in work settings. Created by Tett, Wang, and Fox (2006), the model is based on the work of Salovey and Mayer (1990) and is composed of 144 short items that assess ten distinct facets of emotional intelligence:

1. Recognition of emotion in the self

2. Regulation of emotion in the self

3. Recognition of emotion in others

4. Regulation of emotion in others

5. Non-verbal emotional expression

6. Empathy

7. Intuition versus reason

8. Creative thinking

9. Mood redirected attention

10. Motivating emotions

Best of all, the test can be completed online in only 20 minutes and you are given a comprehensive report on the results.

Feedback

Another method is to use 360-degree feedback. A variety of 360-degree feedback surveys have been around for quite a while. You may be familiar with the concept, but in the workplace they usually focus on a broader approach to performance.

As mentioned previously, 360-degree feedback is a type of survey where feedback is sought from your peers, managers, customers, and people you work with on a regular basis. It's called 360-degree because the perceptions come from a wide circle of your work contacts, giving you a more comprehensive picture than you'd get simply from the standard performance review.

Another advantage of this form of feedback is that in most cases, people are able to give honest and unbiased feedback on an individual's performance.

There are a range of 360-degree tools designed to measure emotional intelligence. I created a 360-degree tool which measures the following five leadership pillars.

The 5 Leadership Pillars

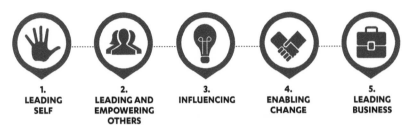

| 1.
LEADING
SELF | 2.
LEADING AND
EMPOWERING
OTHERS | 3.
INFLUENCING | 4.
ENABLING
CHANGE | 5.
LEADING
BUSINESS |

Self-awareness is the key to improving leadership effectiveness. The purpose of this review is to provide further awareness about how participants can have a more significant impact as a leader.

Emotional and Social Competence Inventory (ECI)

This is one of the better-known forms of measurement for EQ. It's a 360-degree survey based on Goleman's model of EQ and it measures 18 competencies grouped into four areas: self-awareness, self-management, social awareness, and relationship management. It focuses on feedback about individual strengths and reveals areas which need improvement.

The survey can be completed by an individual or a team, in case you need to assess the overall capabilities of a group. When done as a team, you can pinpoint weaknesses in group emotional intelligence which could be limiting performance.

The Genos Emotional Intelligence Inventory

This is based on the Genos model of EQ which is a behaviour-based assessment and covers six different areas of competency:

1. Emotional self-awareness

2. Emotional expression

3. Emotional awareness of others

4. Emotional reasoning

5. Emotional self-management and self-control

6. Emotional management of others

While this can be self-assessed, best results come from 360 assessments. It's an online survey which is completed anonymously so team members can be honest in their feedback without fear of reprisal. The survey measures your behaviour in the workplace to discover how often you display emotional intelligence.

Performance Measures

The third approach is to test EQ through performance tests. These involve the kinds of questions you have probably come up against in an interview situation. The reason they are important is because they demonstrate your thinking and your values, and how you apply and communicate them. 'What-would-you-do-if' type questions provoke answers which give insight into your EQ skills in action.

These are of value in recruitment and in developing a team as they give a picture of how each person might operate in your environment.

Practical Assessment

The above are formal tests which have proven successful at assessing EQ, but I don't want to leave it there. I'm a practical person and I want something more tangible to get my hands on. When I assess EQ, my approach is practical as well as data-oriented. Assessing EQ is about more than tools. What matters most about a person's EQ is their application.

Let me remind you of Goleman's model. I believe this is the most practical model to work with from a performance perspective. It breaks down emotional intelligence into four key areas:

1. **Self-awareness** – knowing one's internal states, preferences, resources, and intuitions.

2. **Self-management** – managing one's internal states, impulses, and resources.

3. **Social awareness** – awareness of others' feelings, needs, and concerns.

4. **Relationship management** – skill or adeptness at inducing desirable responses in others.

Two of these areas are internal to the individual but two can be seen by others in interactions, in the way the team works together, and in their results.

Looking for High EQ

What should you look for in a leader's performance or 'on the floor' as signs of high emotional intelligence in action? Below is a three-pronged approach.

Observation will help you to assess social awareness and relationship management.

- Healthy chatter and conversation in the team.

- Team members are willing to collaborate with others or support those members who need help.

- Work is delivered on time and is of a high quality.

- Ideas regularly originate from this team.

- People are comfortable expressing their opinions to the leader and within the team.

- Emotions are acknowledged and respected.

- Leaders deliver good news and bad news with honesty and clarity.

- Leaders and teams have open, transparent and difficult conversions.

- Leaders cope with difficult situations without letting their emotions interfere.

- Focus is on improvement not failures.

- Leaders can pull their teams out of drama or disaster and help them refocus.

- Leaders show empathy and listen to others in meetings and in personal conversations.

- Team members enjoy spending time together even after work.

Connection will create a platform of trust where you can openly discuss the leader's internal states. Don't wait for a standard performance review to dig deep into what's going on. Make the informal open chat a regular part of your process. Ask questions such as:

- How do you feel about that?

- What help do you need?

- Could you have done anything differently?

- What were you thinking/feeling at the time?

Your regular work performance reporting will reflect the results of team performance and work quality. As your leader's EQ increases, you should spot improvements reflected in those reports.

Be Specific. Because EQ is influenced by factors such as age, experience, personality, and situation, it's worth choosing specific competencies to focus on. Choose those which fit with your work culture and values or the specific role you're about to fill.

For example, if yours is a creative business you will need to find leaders who can inspire and nurture creativity in their teams. You might choose to look for competencies which support creativity such as communication, collaboration, and adaptability.

Goleman separates EQ skills into personal and social (or relatable). Under these skills are micro skills. Read each of the skill definitions and note down how you apply each one at the moment.

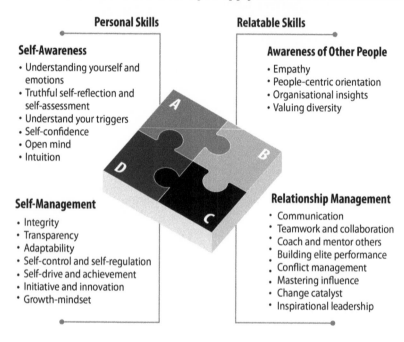

Personal Skills

Self-Awareness
- Understanding yourself and emotions
- Truthful self-reflection and self-assessment
- Understand your triggers
- Self-confidence
- Open mind
- Intuition

Self-Management
- Integrity
- Transparency
- Adaptability
- Self-control and self-regulation
- Self-drive and achievement
- Initiative and innovation
- Growth-mindset

Relatable Skills

Awareness of Other People
- Empathy
- People-centric orientation
- Organisational insights
- Valuing diversity

Relationship Management
- Communication
- Teamwork and collaboration
- Coach and mentor others
- Building elite performance
- Conflict management
- Mastering influence
- Change catalyst
- Inspirational leadership

Self-assessment Skill

Take a skill assessment by rating yourself below. This assessment is a good starting point for reviewing your current level of emotional intelligence. Ensure your appraisal is honest.

Using the table on the following pages, rate your proficiency for each skill (low, medium, high), and the frequency (per cent) at which you practise it. This will help you to identify areas for improvement.

Skills	Description	L	M	H	%
Self-awareness and understanding yourself	Understanding all aspects of your strengths and weaknesses including your emotions, values, motivations, and character, and recognising their impact on both your performance and relationships with others.				
Truthful self-reflection and self-assessment	Identify how well you are able to hold yourself accountable and identify the specific areas for improvement and development.				
Self-confidence	A feeling of trust in your capabilities, perception, and self-worth.				
Open-mindedness	A willingness to be unprejudiced and open to new ideas and ways of working and thinking.				
Intuition	A feeling of knowing or considering something likely based on an instinctive gut feeling as opposed to conscious reasoning.				
Integrity	Being honest and trustworthy and having strong moral and ethical values.				
Transparency	The willingness and ability to operate with honesty and openness.				
Adaptability quotient	The ability to adapt to changes and overcome challenges.				
Emotional self-control and self-regulation	The ability to control disruptive or impulsive emotions and never overreact under stressful conditions.				
Self-drive and achievement	Having the desire and high personal and professional standards to achieve your goals. Holding yourself to a high standard of performance.				

Skills	Description	L	M	H	%
Innovation and initiative	The ability to create, assess, and evaluate independently and to identify opportunities to act and have foresight.				
Growth mindset	The commitment to continuous learning and the desire to constantly become the best version of yourself.				
Empathy	The ability to step into another person's shoes and respond to their feelings and emotions with sensitivity and understanding.				
People-centric orientation	The creation of a friendly environment which honours both customer and team perspectives and considers their emotions and needs.				
Organisational insights	The capacity to understand and analyse the strategies that shape your organisation, including influence, values, power, and internal and external pressures.				
Valuing diversity	The ability to respect and include differences in any area of life and recognise the unique contributions individuals can make with them.				
Communication	The act of conveying clear messages from one source to another; listening to and hearing others; sending and receiving messages accurately.				
Teamwork and collaboration	The fostering of a collaborative environment where teams can work together to achieve a specific goal by sharing ideas and insights.				

Skills	Description	L	M	H	%
Coaching and mentoring others	An advisor's ability to unlock a person's potential, maximise their performance, help them focus on ongoing development, and nurture their abilities in line with their goals.				
Building elite performance	Creating collaborative synergies by pursuing shared goals through teamwork and cooperation, enabling others to improve performance and exceed expectations.				
Conflict management	The ability to manage, negotiate and resolve disagreements, facilitating others to move through conflict.				
Mastering influence	An understanding of human psychology and what excites others to take action, as well as the ability to identify and nurture influential relationships. This requires the ability to strategically steer, powerfully persuade, and inspire commitment in others.				
Change catalyst	The energy and personality that can push others to change their vision and become more enthusiastic.				
Inspirational leadership	The power to energise and motivate individuals to strive for their goals and inspire them to bring change by polishing their skills.				

CHAPTER FOUR

Developing Self-awareness – Knowing Yourself: A Revolution of Authenticity

"Many leadership problems are driven by low self-awareness"
— Bill Hybels

Self-awareness is the Road to Knowing Yourself

Knowing yourself is the starting point for growth and effective leadership because it's the foundation upon which social and emotional intelligence is built. If you don't build a house on strong foundations, the house will collapse. The same principle applies here.

Knowing yourself is the precursor of authenticity. When you're self-aware, you act and interact in an authentic way and people can relate to you.

We can't develop emotional self-control, empathy, teamwork, or leadership skills until we become aware of our feelings and how they influence our thoughts and behaviours. Being aware of yourself will also help you link your emotions and responses to the effectiveness of your interactions with others.

Self-awareness is the ability to objectively evaluate yourself and to question your instincts, patterns, and assumptions. The capacity to reflect and trust your own self-assessment requires maturity and habitual critical self-reflection.

As mentioned in earlier chapters, the best leaders are self-aware; it's one of the most critical skills for leaders to develop. A study by Korn Ferry found that when organisations have leaders and employees with a higher level of self-awareness, they demonstrate stronger performance.

Defensiveness drives negative behaviour. When leaders act defensively without self-awareness, they don't realise the harm they're causing, as they lose the ability to think rationally.

Example – Chris

I once worked with an executive, Chris. Chris is a hard-working, ambitious individual. He was recently promoted into a senior position in a new organisation, after a long stint in an environment that didn't allow him to thrive. It was his first role at the next executive level. He was doubting his abilities and feeling a little overwhelmed because he wanted to prove himself, both of which are normal feelings. More than 70 per cent of people feel this way when stepping into more senior roles.

One morning, only a few months into his new role, Chris received an email about losing a large piece of business he'd been banking on to hit his end of financial year targets. Chris and his team lost the project to one of their biggest competitors. He had included his project as guaranteed on his sales forecast but neglected to manage risk or consider he might lose the bid. He was confident that he'd secured the project and as a result he did not build an alternative pipeline of opportunity. With great trepidation, Chris communicated the problem to his senior partner, who asked for an explanation.

When Chris's senior partner requested an explanation, Chris was anxious to meet expectations, and fearful of how he would be perceived. Instead of taking responsibility, he chose to throw one of his peers under the bus, blaming them for his mistakes.

As the partner reflected on Chris's actions, both recent and previous, he recognised a competitive and defensive behavioural pattern. Chris came to me having been instructed to seek support to change his behaviour and improve his accountability, integrity, and relationships.

It's hard to trust a person who is unable to consider the bigger picture or other perspectives. In being defensive and blaming others, Chris showed his inability to take responsibility, which would have required humility. Humility is something many of us avoid due to fear of failure and being judged or hurt. Defensive people avoid it like the plague. It's a trait they're afraid to show.

For Chris, there was plenty of opportunity for growth. As mentioned earlier, EQ is one of the tops skills cited as a non-negotiable for future leaders, and he was serious about becoming an impactful and visionary leader. Self-awareness was the starting point and I'm pleased to share that Chris is now a highly respected leader.

Chris's story isn't unusual; it's normal for us to feel defensive every now and then, some more than others. Great leaders always welcome feedback. They are open to ongoing improvements. If you respectfully approach a leader with feedback, they'll listen.

Team Perspective

Being a leader is about self-awareness, perspective, and learning to become a better version of yourself. The starting point for development is awareness.

Great leaders are responsible for their team and know they're only as good as the people around them. They're constantly aware of what's going on and part of that awareness concerns their team's perspective of them.

But what about the bosses who are not open to understanding other perspectives of them, or different perspectives in general? I've been researching the impact for years in my work with hundreds of leaders, and a lack of awareness impacts performance.

Example - Team Perspective

I witnessed one of my coaching clients dictating what he wanted to his executive team. He didn't want to hear their thoughts or allow for their contributions. When I pointed this out to him in private to help with awareness, he became defensive. He was not open to considering other people's perspectives and lacked awareness around this impediment. He was not capable of changing his behaviour because he refused to consider the impact of his actions. As a result, he began to lose his top executive team because he continued to lead through a comment-and-control style.

Understanding how others perceive you is another critical element of self-awareness. Great leaders are willing to change and adapt, they're life-long learners and practitioners and they know that self-awareness is fundamental for personal growth.

Great leaders such as Steve Jobs and Richard Branson know the importance of empowering people and not limiting their performance.

"It doesn't make sense to hire smart people and tell them what to do; we hire smart people so that they can tell us what to do."
- Steve Jobs

"I surround myself with people who have knowledge and talents in areas where I might not be so well versed."
- Richard Branson

When you consider how aware these incredible leaders are, it's no wonder they have succeeded. They know exactly what aspects they are lacking in and have hired people who can help them succeed. Plus, they've spent time on their own personal and professional development.

Once a leader sheds that defensive outer layer and becomes vulnerable and adaptable to change, they can look inwards at what they can and cannot do. These gaps can then be filled with both the ongoing development of their own skills and by employing well-trained people they trust, who will then take their businesses to new heights.

Exercise – Being Aware of Defensive Behaviour

Before you can look inwards and consider the areas you need to develop, it's important to be aware of and able to manage (and identify in others) a defensive response. To help you out, I have prepared some straightforward steps:

- ❏ Identify the physical signs related to intensified emotions. These include rapid heart rate, high charge of energy in the body, tight stomach, and hot sweaty skin.

- ❏ Identify the behavioural warning signs such as wanting to be right all the time, wanting the last word, continuing to defend, and pushing information to prove your point.

- ❏ Identify the need to blame exhibited by being critical of others or mind reading.

❐ Manage your emotions by taking time out to calm down. Use that time to reflect and reframe your thinking. Remember that your thoughts are not reality; recognise when you're mind reading. Instead of thinking, "I'm a failure", or worse, "I'm going to look stupid, because I've made a mistake", you can think, "Let's find a solution, problems are opportunities after all."

❐ Focus on the problem, not the people. This allows solutions to be found. If you don't know how to fix something, simply say you will work on finding a solution. Excuses don't help.

❐ Reflect on situations and interactions with people. Consider how you could improve in the future.

Day by day, if you implement these steps towards self-awareness, you will find your behaviour changing for the better. It may be difficult at first, but once it becomes a learnt behaviour, there's no going back. You'll be a leader to be reckoned with.

Example – I've Been There Before

There was a point early on in my career; an employee accused me of bullying in the workplace. It was one of the most challenging times in my career, and I didn't want to take responsibility at the time. In meetings, I would trigger an individual's defence mechanisms, and when he became defensive, I'd become defensive too. I was young and still learning. I'd not even heard of EQ in leadership or how to navigate and influence through understanding human behaviour. I tried to blame the other person. He was underperforming, and my approach was to performance manage him. With hindsight, I see I could have done more to support him in improving his performance. Luckily, I was open to self-reflection and self-awareness, which led me to understand that as the leader, it was my responsibility to set this person up for success, and my approach was not achieving that. I just wanted results; I wanted to prove myself to my superiors to earn a promotion. I was operating from a place of self-interest, not a place of servant leadership. In the end, he requested a transfer to another department, after the organisation investigated his claims and found no basis for his accusations.

I've been one of the lucky ones, an escapee of sorts, because over the last couple of decades I've challenged the old-school management thinking to redefine leadership in a more effective way. It has made me happier and had a more positive impact on people and results.

Self-awareness is not only crucial for leadership, it's essential in everyday life because it informs you of who you are as a person and how you relate to this big bad world.

Exercise – Reflection Time

I've suggested including reflection time in your day. This might mean:

1. Thinking about how people reacted to you, not just as their boss but as an influential leader.

2. Considering how connected you were while working with or managing others.

Remember, the key is to be honest. You don't need to share this with anyone else so tell yourself the truth. That's where you'll find room to grow.

The Importance of Feedback

Have you ever had a 360 review? As mentioned in the previous chapter, in a 360, both your peers and your managers anonymously provide feedback on all aspects of your behaviour. The 360-assessment system that I've developed reviews all the fundamental leadership pillars within the self-leadership, leading others, and leading business categories.

A large study by Tasha Eurich (2018) collected data findings in the thousands which confirmed that leaders who searched for feedback on how they could improve were more self-aware and more accomplished compared to those who pursued only positive feedback.

I was only able to advance my career to CEO level thanks to my ability and willingness to be self-aware. It has helped me to discover and master the areas I needed to develop.

In summary, self-awareness is not a new concept, and most successful leaders will say that it is one of the keys to career success.

"Knowing yourself is the
beginning of all wisdom."
- Aristotle

Don't be fooled; self-awareness is difficult to master. Unfortunately, when it comes to self-awareness, there's no one-size-fits-all answer. The only person who can teach you self-awareness is YOU, although you can enlist help to expedite the process.

> "There are three things extremely hard:
> steel, a diamond, and to know one's self."
> - Benjamin Franklin

Right now, self-reflection is a practice that you can use to further develop your self-awareness and discover how to be the best version of yourself. Self-reflection is also a practice which will help keep at bay the dreadful imposter syndrome that plagues so many high achievers. A study by a Harvard Business School professor found people were more in control, capable and confident when they spent time reflecting daily. As with any habit, self-reflection is all about consistency.

Exercise – Answer These Questions

A good start to strengthening your self-awareness is to answer the following questions.

- **?** What values do I operate with, and how do I want to show up?

- **?** What quality do I admire most about myself?

- **?** What do I want to be known for?

- **?** What is my biggest weakness?

- **?** What is my biggest strength?

? What are the three words that best describe me?

? When do I perform at my best?

? When I'm thinking negatively, how do I turn those thoughts around?

? When I feel overwhelmed, how do I remain in control?

? How can I be a better leader?

? Where have I let myself down as a leader?

? What motivates me to perform at my best?

? What's my definition of success?

? How do I make a decision; by intuition or logical analysis?

? What is the biggest 'what if' on my mind?

? What are the key areas I'd like to focus on to improve?

? Are there any areas of my life that stress me out?

? What makes me angry?

? What makes me afraid?

? How am I perceived by my colleagues and peers?

The fact is that we operate the majority of our thoughts and actions on autopilot. Our habits, instincts, and reactions carry us through life and we don't stop to become aware of how we operate.

People can operate in defence with no idea that this might be a problem for them, hindering their job performance, career success, and leadership effectiveness. Knowing who we are and how we're seen is critical to our success.

Self-awareness starts from within, and a person with self-awareness thinks about and reflects on their actions and behaviours. They might think, "Hmm... I had a bad day at work, so I reached for a bottle of wine when I got home. Perhaps this is a trigger"; an individual who lacks self-awareness just hits the bottle and doesn't look back.

I've worked with and studied people who made transformational changes in their self-awareness. It takes courage, commitment, and humility. Self-improvement is a personal choice—what will you choose?

CHAPTER FIVE

Becoming a Thought Leader – Coming to Grips with Authority and Executive Presence

The most widely accepted definition of 'thought leader' is by Joel Kurtzman, Editor-in-Chief of *Strategy & Business*, who said:

"A thought leader is recognized by peers,
customers and industry experts as someone
who deeply understands the business they
are in, the needs of their customers and the
broader marketplace in which they operate.
They have distinctively original ideas,
unique points of view and new insights."

Being recognised as a thought leader doesn't happen overnight. It's not the result of one great idea. To become a thought leader, you need that wonderful combination of authority, executive presence, and originality, and you need a strategy behind you. Have you got what it takes to become a thought leader?

Let's dive right in and focus on developing your authority and executive presence, then I'll show you how to develop a strategy to build on those and become the thought leader in your industry.

Why Look at Authority and Presence?

Authority and presence are factors which distinguish a thought leader from the pack, but what do those factors look like and how can you develop them? Before I move on, I want to dispel a couple of myths.

Firstly, when you read about authority and presence, it's usually with terms like X factor, star quality, or charisma. While they undoubtedly apply, those descriptions really don't help if you're trying to build your own authority and executive presence. They don't give you anything to get a grip on. The myth turns authority and presence into magical traits that appear to be out of reach for normal people. Furthermore, you certainly don't need to be a charismatic, extroverted leader to develop authority and presence. Plenty of introverted leaders have developed authority and presence, Warren Buffet, Albert Einstein, Elon Musk and Barack Obama, to name a few.

The second myth I often hear is that those who have it were born with it. That's simply wrong. The truth is, anyone can build their authority and develop executive presence if they work at it.

I'd like to take a closer look at authority and executive presence because while you can have authority without having presence, the reverse is not true. To be a thought leader you need to have both.

What is Authority and What Does it Look Like?

A particular client of mine was an executive who managed a senior leader called Robyn, who managed a small team. She admired Robyn and had believed she had potential.

One day, my client found Robyn crying in the women's bathroom, bad-mouthing to one of her team members. She had just been passed over for a promotion because she had not taken the time to develop her critical leadership skills, even though the company had paid for her to receive coaching.

My client was disappointed in Robyn, not because she was crying but because she felt the need to hide away, as though she was ashamed. She'd also heard Robyn was bad-mouthing her and the company. It altered her opinion of Robyn immediately although she didn't realise that until much later. Despite remaining at the same senior level as the other leaders, Robyn had lost her authority with both peers and team.

There are two kinds of authority: the kind that comes as part of your role, and the kind that's given to you by the people who matter. Of course, Robyn should be able to express her emotions and her disappointment to her team; that's part of being authentic as a leader. The real issue when it comes to maintaining authority is expressing it in a professional manner.

In other words, authority is as much about image and presentation as it is about expertise. It's more than any X factor because it's an organic authority (not a position of power), coupled with authenticity, and backed up with knowledge.

What is Presence and What Does it Look Like?

When you look around a room, you'll recognise those with presence and those without. You'll notice who people are watching and paying attention to. You'll see which person seems to gather a crowd. Sometimes you'll even notice a slight hush fall over the room when someone enters. These are all signs of a person with presence.

People with presence look confident, calm, and composed. When they speak, people listen intently. John Baldoni, author and leadership educator, describes presence like this:

"Presence is the radiance of authenticity.
That is, you radiate sincerity and you have what it takes to make good things happen. It is different from charisma; charisma is a gift, but it's the sheen on metal. Presence is the real deal – a person's mettle."

Put simply, presence is about your ability to inspire confidence and commitment and to gain trust. It inspires people to pay attention and follow you. It opens doors and helps develop connections critical to your goals and career advancement. At its heart are excellent communication and relationship skills. Executive presence is the ability to step out of the usual limitations in search of new solutions, and have your team fully on side, happy to take the risk with you.

What Has Authority Got to Do with Presence?

Authority and executive presence go together. Presence without authority is just window dressing. I remember years ago being inspired by a leader and following her because she'd filled me with confidence. My belief was shattered when we reached a crossroad and she couldn't make a necessary decision. I felt she'd promised something she couldn't deliver. She had presence but no authority.

A report by Dr Gavin Dagley (2013) called 'Executive Presence: Influence Beyond Authority' investigated the qualities defining executive presence and summarised it like this:

> **"**
> "Effective leadership causes people to act; effective executive presence causes people to listen and act."

Authority tells people what to do. Executive presence makes people pay attention. Once you have learnt to capture attention, you're ready to start presenting yourself as a thought leader.

Professor Peter Hawkins developed the API Trust model (Authority, Presence, Impact), which describes the interrelationship between authority and presence. Here is a visual of the connection between authority, presence and getting things done.

- **Authority – Based on your past.** This relates to what you know, your experiences, your track record, your achievements, your qualifications, and your status.

- **Presence – Based on your now.** This is about being in the present, building relationships, establishing rapport, understanding situations, and having high emotional intelligence. It's about standing by your ethics and convictions despite pressure to conform to lesser standards.

- **Impact – Based on your future.** This is what you want to achieve. It's about your ability to influence thoughts and behaviours, lead change, and guide others towards a goal.

At the heart of authority, presence and impact is confidence, which is earned through a blend of all three. This is the sweet spot, and foundation of your position as thought leader.

How to Build Your Authority

Are you a quiet achiever? Do people know how good you are at what you do? If they don't, you won't be able to claim any level of authority. If you want to lead effectively, this is something you need to change.

The aim here is to increase your credibility and there are several ways you can do this. These suggestions won't suit everyone, so select the techniques applicable to your work situation.

1. **Make sure you have the right skills and knowledge in place and keep updated.** Not only is this important for gaining trust in your alleged capabilities, it's the basis for your necessary confidence going forward.

2. **Volunteer to lead a task force.** Breaking new ground is challenging and not everyone will be up for it. There is always a need for someone to lead the process. By taking the helm, you prove your leadership's worth and potentially create a ground-breaking new system or solution you can lay claim to, along with your team, of course.

3. **Share your advice.** Be open and willing to share your knowledge with those who need it.

Speak Up

If you're doing nothing besides focusing on your continuous development, you deserve to be speaking up for yourself. If you have the skills or experience needed, say so! I know this can be difficult, particularly for women to do, considering the level of modesty drilled into us. However, when there's a situation that needs what you can offer, you have a moral duty to speak up.

How can you speak up about your abilities without feeling like you're bragging or wasting your time? I have two tips for you:

1. Never use modifiers such as 'perhaps', 'just', and 'might'. They immediately reduce your authority and suggests a lack of self-confidence. Maximising modifiers also imply hesitation, an example "I'm definitely ready to deliver my speech" sounds weaker than "I'm ready to deliver my speech". No one will believe in you if you don't believe in yourself.

2. Keep the emotion out of it. Keeping communication factual and concise removes any impression of bragging. Applying your experience to a situation can keep the focus on the task at hand while boosting your perceived authority. This is a simple way to present yourself as an expert without having to worry about seeming pushy.

How to Build Your Executive Presence

While executive presence as a term is hard to define, we know it springs from a set of skills which can be learnt.

You'll need:

- Leadership skills and strong authority, inspire action.

- Self-confidence to encourage others to have confidence in you.

- Self-awareness to understand and manage your own behaviours and take responsibility for your actions and results.

- Great communication skills to help you speak clearly, persuasively, and in a way that meets the needs of your team.

Most of your executive presence will be demonstrated through your communication skills, especially in the way you handle problems, lead your team, and manage their emotional needs. Most of all, it will show in your ability and willingness to share your authentic self with others. If you're ready to start building or improving your executive presence, you'll need to work on these skills:

1. **Look the part**. I remember being told, "Dress not for the position you have now, but for the position you want to achieve". The same concept applies here. It's all about being credible, and showing up with your shirt untucked damages your credibility. First impressions really matter.

   Dress and act the part. Study and practice the characteristics of leaders you admire. Stand straight and strong, look people in the eye, and speak clearly.

2. **Know your value.** If you don't know your real value to your company, it's time to start discovering it. You bring a unique attitude and skill set to your role. Work out what you do well, what makes you different to others, what you can do that others can't, and how your special combination of talents makes a difference to your team and your workplace. Ask your mentors and teammates for their opinions because they will see things in you that

you won't see in yourself. Have on hand a few examples of your achievements for when the opportunity arises for you to provide proof of your value.

3. **Learn to give yourself time.** Leaders with high executive presence never appear to be rushed; they are calm and composed. They aren't afraid of silence and will pause to think before speaking or acting. They present their words with careful consideration which inspires confidence. Remember, you don't have to have all the answers. Give yourself time to think before you speak or act, and you'll look confident and composed even in times of stress.

4. **Polish your listening skills.** Peter Drucker said, "The most important thing in communication is hearing what isn't said." Learn to listen beyond the spoken words. Ask questions if you feel there's more going on. Look people in the eye as they speak so they know you are engaged. Listening is more than courtesy; it's establishing a trust relationship as well as information gathering. With good listening, you establish with the speaker that you value their words, which encourages their openness and commitment to you, as well as building their motivation.

5. **Stand for something and decide what you want to be known for.** Share your vision of what you're working towards. Share your 'why' so people gain insight into your personal values. Allow your vision and values to flow through your work so others see it in action. If I ask you why you're so keen to improve your executive presence, I guarantee you won't say, "Simply to be a better leader"; there's more to it than that. Why do you want to

be a better leader? No doubt your answer would involve doing something for someone else or improving a specific situation. Dig deep into your choices and be clear on what is driving you. Your vision and values are inspirational.

6. **Organically step up into your next level role.** This is along the same lines as dressing not for the position you have now, but for the position you want. When people see you step up, they assume it is your role, and you soon assume the role. Consider the skills and responsibility necessary for the role you wish to obtain. What are you missing? How do you cross-train or get involved more?

7. **Set your boundaries.** People with executive presence will say no when they need to. They are aware of their own value and don't feel the need to people-please. They know their priorities and stick with them.

8. **Build your network.** Having a network is always useful but if you want to build your authority and presence, it's vital. Having a solid network helps you understand and work with the politics built into every organisation. It helps you get things done. Knowing the right people is useful but remember: a sound network is based on real relationships and connection, not just a list of contacts. This is something you will need to constantly work on, but the payoff is worthwhile. Stay in touch with people, connect often, speak up to ensure you have a voice, and freely offer your help when you can. That's how you'll gain the confidence and respect of your network.

Know Yourself

Here are the real keys to executive presence and great leadership. Be real. Be authentic. While you can gain all the skills which make up executive presence, they won't work without a sound foundation. Being open and honest can be daunting, which is why many leaders are closed books. This is understandable; when you open yourself up, you're exposed to criticism which can hurt.

That's why self-awareness is so important. It gives you the maturity to manage your emotions and response to every situation so you can focus instead on handling it constructively. Whether you call it being self-aware or mindful, it's about being present in the moment. When you are present you pick up a lot more of what's happening in front of you – data you can use to formulate your response. Being aware of your thoughts and feelings, and managing your reaction helps you make the most of every situation.

Your unique combination of body language, appearance, talents, experience, communication skills, and character create your presence. It's up to you to capitalise on those attributes to create the presence you want.

Nine Steps to Build Your Thought Leadership Strategy

Every credible thought leader has a strategy behind them, and they've put in the hard work to get where they are. More importantly, they are genuine in their willingness to share their thinking and to help others solve problems or find new solutions. They believe in what they do and love to talk about their topic for the good of their people. If this isn't you, no strategy will help you become a recognised thought leader.

With all the work you've done to build your authority and presence, you've laid some great groundwork. Let's incorporate that into building a long-term strategy which will position you as a thought leader.

Prepare

1. Define your current self.

> **?** Where are you now?

> **?** What are you known for?

> **?** What is your expertise?

> **?** What do you want to be known for?

> **?** Are there any image or reputation issues you need to overcome before you can move on?

2. Define your stance.

> **?** What do you stand for or against?

> **?** What do you want to change by becoming a thought leader?

> **?** What help do you want to be able to offer people?

3. Gather information.

> **?** What are the key issues in your industry or niche right now?

? What is the media talking about?

? Find out what your clients what to know. What questions are they asking? What information or ideas are they missing?

? Research the best place to connect with your target audience. What do they read? Where do they hang out? Where do they currently go for help?

Take Action

4. Start writing.

☐ Create quality content, targeting current topics.

☐ Write informative or inquisitive articles discussing ideas around the key issues facing your industry.

☐ Create articles or social media posts which meet your clients' need for answers.

☐ Extend your writing beyond information and discuss new approaches. Shake things up. Don't be afraid to disrupt the status quo.

☐ Start an industry-level conversation. This establishes your position and expertise.

☐ Use current events as a stimulus for your writing so you're presenting newsworthy content which you can submit to magazines.

- ❒ Write a press release on a topical issue including quotes from yourself to position you as an authority and thought leader.

5. Present your content in different formats.

- ❒ Publish a blog.

- ❒ Create a podcast.

- ❒ Record a video.

- ❒ Present in Facebook Live.

- ❒ Develop quality posts for social media both for research purposes (gathering information) and offering thought provoking content.

6. Find influencers and work with them.

- ❒ Comment on their material.

- ❒ Volunteer to help them.

- ❒ Attend networking events.

- ❒ Share their useful articles.

7. Become a speaker on your authority topic.

- ❒ Pitch your presentation to conference organisers or the media, outlining your proposed topic, what you intend to cover, and how it will meet the demands of their attendees.

- [ ] Don't forget to include a bio which reveals why you are qualified to speak on the topic.

- [ ] Most importantly, make sure your topic is current and newsworthy, and don't just rehash what everyone else is saying.

8. Write case studies.

- [ ] Not only are these useful to include in articles, they are a clear way to explain how you developed your expertise and prove it at the same time.

- [ ] Case studies are a great memory jogger when you're looking for information to support your position or explanation.

9. Write about your experience.

- [ ] Whether it's submitting an article to an industry publication or to your internal newsletter, people love to learn about the challenges you've faced and tackled.

- [ ] Remember, you don't always have to have been successful to find a lesson to share. Your humility and willingness to share openly will only add to your credibility.

Strive to always be adding value to the conversation rather than attention seeking or filling conversational voids. In summary, produce timely content which presents alternative ways of thinking and share it readily, maintaining focus on your thought leadership and clarity about who you strive to be. You can see how much work is involved in becoming a thought leader and why it's not an overnight goal. However, if you want to be a thought leader, you will do the work with pleasure. Start examining your thought processes now and give them a shake-up. You'll need to be innovative and creative to stand out.

PART II

LEADING OTHERS

CHAPTER SIX

———

Empathy – Linking Human Behaviour, Performance, Power, and Action

Empathy is Key

What is hindering our ability to create elite performance? I believe it's a lack of empathy and let me tell you why. An organisation led by someone who lacks empathy is bound to fail, particularly in the future, where the skills of today become archaic (in years and months, not decades). Our tomorrow is so profoundly different, that we can't begin to imagine it.

As mentioned throughout this book, the Fifth Industrial Revolution will soon be upon us, and it will demand leaders 'human up'. The growth of AI is making soft skills progressively more important, as these are skills robots can't automate. Emotional intelligence is high on the list of skills in demand, and in mastering influence our focus is on empathy.

In old-school management theory, empathy might have been classified as soft, perhaps even as the responsibility of the human resources division. You might have even seen empathy printed as an organisational 'value' on a flyer, implying an interest beyond the bottom line. In both circumstances, the spirit of empathy becomes diminished, and its power dismissed.

Why is empathy essential in business? Daniel Goleman, who is a world-renowned expert on empathy and emotional intelligence in the workplace, shares just how vital it is:

"Without it, a person can have the best training in the world, a brilliant analytical mind, and an endless supply of smart ideas, but he still won't make a great leader."

My teachers and peers told me I wouldn't amount to anything. No one understood what I was going through at home, growing up with a mother who was an addict; a mother who provided little or no primary care. No one wanted to take the time to consider why I wasn't doing well. Therein lies the problem; no one in the education system cared beyond their own self-interest. There was a lack of empathy and compassion, which was consistent across all industries back then. With sheer drive and determination, I broke free from this adversity. I built my career, and although the path was non-linear each turn in the road enriched my knowledge, perspective, and adaptability. I went from homeless teenager to CEO. It took many years, a bucket load of hard work, and a lot of mistakes, the biggest, was conforming to the established corporate cultures which suppressed the expression of emotion. The pressure to conform to organisationally appropriate behaviour was intense, plus the need to appear competent and in control meant I became robotic and void of feeling. Luckily for me, I challenged the status quo and decided that approach was limiting people's potential, including mine. I chose to lead the way, for change, EQ and empathy became essential tools in my leadership toolbox during times of transformational organisational change. It allowed me to deliver substantial growth during the global financial crisis when most of our competitors declined. Nowadays, many organisations and leaders realise that empathy serves a purpose, to engage, lead, innovate, collaborate, to reduce conflict, to communicate better, and to lead an organisation to succeed. Empathy and EQ are no longer the black sheep of leadership; they are the vital skills required for leaders to thrive in the future.

Why Empathy?

Empathy enables us to connect as humans and helps you to understand if you've connected with the people you're trying to reach. I share an example later in this chapter which demonstrates how empathy helps you to predict the potential effects your decisions and actions will have on others, so you can strategise and prepare accordingly. Empathy, at its core, is the ability to put yourself in another person's shoes and understand their perspective, experience, and feelings.

Operating with empathy is not a top priority in corporate cultures, nor is it for many leaders. This is thanks to factors such as old-school management, unconscious incompetence, and ego. I genuinely believe that people don't know what they don't know, and as we evolve, the skills in demand change. Without a doubt, empathy is a critical skill in demand for the future of leadership.

Influencing

Influencing is an art; a learned skill which doesn't come easily to everyone. To influence successfully, you must appeal to both the head and the heart. You must make a connection, identify triggers, and adapt your communication style to mirror those you are trying to influence so they feel comfortable and trust you. It can take time to develop empathy and awareness, which are crucial skills for mastering influence.

When you master influencing, people will treat interactions with you as though you're a visionary thinker and legendary persuader just like Richard Branson and Steve Jobs. If you've not mastered influencing techniques as a leader, you can waste hours and hours going around in a circle getting nowhere fast. If you don't learn to influence, you will quickly be forgotten.

People who influence are unstoppable. They share big ideas; win people over; create empowered, accountable teams; exude executive presence; and stand out as successful leaders who get results.

When you become a master influencer, you're capable of powerfully persuading, strategically steering, and inspiring commitment. This capacity results in the creation of trust, empowerment, and accountability in others, which in turn deliver elite performance and results. But before we can tackle mastering influence, we must first get empathy right.

Why Do Leaders Neglect Empathy?

While there are many factors at play, research by a social psychologist at the University of California, Dacher Keltner, concluded that observed studies show people with power suffer gaps in empathy. In addition, research from Sukhvinder Obhi, a neuroscientist, indicated power has the ability to change how the brain functions. Therefore, neglecting empathy is correlated with power, ego, staying in our comfort zones, and conscious incompetence, to name a few.

Ego

Ego is our self-perception and how we want to be seen by the outside world. Everyone has an ego; it's the natural side of our humanity. However, there is a scale with ego and humility, as illustrated below, and at any moment in time we can go up and down the scale.

This can be exemplified with a comparison between two recent presidents of the United States, Barack Obama and Donald Trump. At one end of the scale is a president who operated with humility, and on the other is one who predominately operates on the opposite side of the spectrum.

It is possible to operate at both ends of the scale at any given moment. If we delve into character types, you can see which end people belong, but it's not fixed; people can decide to operate more at one end than the other. It's a choice.

> "More the knowledge lesser the ego,
> lesser the knowledge more the ego"
> - Albert Einstein

Ego tends to align with a sense of self-confidence and can therefore be triggered as a human defence mechanism. This is an important aspect to understand because in future chapters we'll be covering how people are triggered, and how you can be strategic in helping to disarm people before they become triggered.

Ego is a focus on self, and empathy is a focus on others, so ego does not align well with empathy. You can't drive and close your eyes at the same time, can you? Unfortunately, many leaders stay down the ego end of the scale too much and it hinders their capacity to genuinely empathise with others. This, my friend, is one of our biggest problems. You need to be able to move.

The political arena within organisations shaped by the hierarchical power structure encourages egotistical behaviour which serves no one.

Comfort Zone

Our brains are hard-wired to respond to challenging situations with fight or flight mode, and we're fundamentally wired to prefer to remain in our comfort zones. Think about the nervous feeling you get when you're preparing to make a speech or present to your superiors. Perhaps your hands begin to sweat or your heart begins to race; this is your fight or flight mode kicking into action. When we're out of our comfort zones, we feel *un*comfortable. Sometimes empathising with others takes you outside your comfort zone, you may feel incredibly vulnerable because you no longer feel in control. When you master empathy and influence, you're in complete control.

People within organisations, particularly long-standing organisations that have exercised old-school management practices for a long time, are in comfortable environments. To step outside of that is to challenge the status quo, which is a necessary move if you want to rise above everyone else and become a leader. After all, insanity is doing the same thing over and over again but expecting different results.

Unconscious Incompetence

Everyone has the opportunity to reach their full potential, and your potential is not pre-determined, as some social norms may have you believe (I would have been a hopeless case if my starting position had dictated the rest of my journey). I have witnessed people promoted further than their level of skills and competence should theoretically have allowed. These people don't attempt to gain the necessary knowledge, perhaps because they believe they already have the essential skills. This creates a perpetual cycle of unconscious incompetence as we learn from leaders who are not good role models. I believe this is another big problem now because many of our leaders are self-serving and lacking in empathy, which limits the potential for elite performance. Empathy is, indeed, the starting point for building great elite performance teams.

How Do You Learn Empathy in Leadership?

All learning and growth begin with awareness. Awareness begins with consciousness around our thought and decision-making processes. How we manage our emotions, talk to ourselves, and communicate with and influence others are necessary building blocks.

Research conducted by Harvard Business Review (2018) shows that only 10 to 15 per cent of people are self-aware, revealing that the majority of people are not aware of how they are operating. This leaves space for leaders who are master influencers to stand out and make an impact.

Clever businesses have achieved sustainable growth, solid market performance, and innovative change by operating with empathy and consideration for their people, both employees and clients. Psychologists note there are three different types of empathy: cognitive, emotional, and compassionate.

Cognitive (Thinking) Empathy

Thinking empathy is better described as 'a different perspective,' and it's not what most people think of when they think of empathy.

It's the ability to put yourself in someone else's shoes and see from their perspective, and it's one of the most useful skills in influencing others. It lets you understand someone else's perspective without feeling their emotions. It's a logical process, so for those leaders whose style is logical, this is a skill that can be tapped into quickly.

Thinking empathy, as opposed to feeling empathy, has a bit of a dark side because as Daniel Goleman, author of Emotional

Intelligence, notes, "A torturer needs this ability if only to calibrate his cruelty better."

Working with executives, the first stage of developing empathy tends to concern cognitive empathy, as they can step into other people's shoes without experiencing a feeling of compassion. I'm sure most of you would understand compassion is the crucial part of genuinely leveraging empathy when mastering influencing. But cognitive empathy is a basic first step and can be a stage where most leaders remain for a long time.

Emotional (Feeling) Empathy

Emotional empathy is where you can read, sense and feel the emotions of others as they're feeling them. It is vital in leadership because it enables you to identify, understand, and experience other people's feelings. As babies, we experience emotional empathy as one of our first emotions. When a mother tickles her baby, laughing and smiling as she does so, the baby senses her emotion and responds by mirroring it.

Emotional empathy has a dark side too because you can become overwhelmed by other people's emotions and therefore unable to respond constructively. Psychologists have coined the term 'empath' which they use to describe a sensitive individual who experiences a high level of empathy; often, these individuals take on pain of others at their own expense. It's known as 'empathy overload'. Those with a tendency to become overwhelmed need to become better at managing their own emotions. They do this through focusing on self-regulation and self-control. In my experience, empaths don't make great leaders because their empathy causes overwhelm and holds them back from making tough decisions.

Compassionate (Thinking and Feeling) Empathy

Compassionate empathy means feeling what others are feeling and taking the necessary action to support or help them. In leadership, compassionate empathy is the type of empathy used most frequently, as it's about leveraging the benefits of each kind of empathy to mitigate problems.

Example – Sarah

Years ago, on my last day in an organisation, a woman, Sarah, approached me and said, "I remember the first time you asked me to come into your office. At first, I was scared, but it turned out to be a day that changed my life."

Sarah talked about how dedicated she was when she first started with the company. She was at the office early every day because she loved her work, and she was happy in every aspect of her life.

Then one day, she started to feel miserable. She found it hard to get out of bed every day. She was crying for no apparent reason, she felt like a failure and that life was not worth living. She felt like a shell of herself, and not one of her colleagues noticed.

She went on to say, "You walked past me, you were on your way to the bathroom. Before you turned the corner, you stopped and looked at me. Your serious look scared the life out of me. You continued into the bathroom, but when you returned you asked me to come into your office.

In your office, you asked me if I was okay. You were the only person who saw that I needed help, and you convinced me to let you call and make an appointment with my doctor.

Your intervention changed my life. I've not told you just how important that day was for me, but now that you're leaving, I had to tell you that you've been a person who's had a positive impact on my life and I'm going to miss you."

Here's the truth: I had never realised the full power of empathy and compassion until that moment. It was transformative for me to hear how I'd been an incredibly important person in Sarah's life because I didn't even think it was a big deal.

This is a very personal and extreme case of empathy and compassion in the workplace but, upon reflection, Sarah sharing her perspective with me helped me improve and become a more empathetic leader.

In leadership, people generally don't need you to feel their pain. In this case, I didn't need to cry alongside Sarah in my office that day (emotional empathy). To be the best version of a leader you can be, people don't just need you to understand their perspective (thinking empathy). Instead, they need you to show genuine compassion and understanding. It's about finding some truth in other people's perspective, though you don't have to agree with it. The essential element of compassionate empathy is ensuring the necessary action is taken to resolve the issue.

Example – John

A client, the MD of a privately owned organisation in London, received an offer to merge with a global company. The MD and other directors had decided to proceed with the merger, but at the final stages of negotiation, one director showed resistance and started to hold up the process. The MD sought my support. I asked the MD, "Why is the director (John) holding back now?"

The MD responded, "John says it's because he doesn't believe the company is a good fit, and we should remain independent."

His colleagues assume this is the problem, and they try to convince John that he's wrong. However, it's not the fundamental problem and they're not going to influence him until they frame how his perspective fits.

I ask the MD to tell me what motivates John; what drives him. He said, "John likes to achieve. He wants to work independently and he likes to be in control."

"Okay, so how is he feeling right now, based on what drives him?"

"He feels… uncertain", the MD answered.

Now we're talking!

Using cognitive empathy, we can now understand John's perspective. However, without compassionate empathy we can't influence him to move towards the desired outcome in which he's genuinely on board with the merger.

Initially, the diagnosis for John's concern was that he'd prefer the organisation remained independent because the company was not a good fit.

The application of cognitive empathy and compassion enables a better understanding of John's true issues and concerns. Ultimately the problem is John's uncertainty about his place and future if the companies merge. He's an achiever who prefers to work autonomously and he's worried that he won't have the same level of freedom.

I asked the MD, "How do you show John certainty?" The MD replied, "I'll tell him the company is a good fit for us culturally, and I don't know why he's slowing down the merger."

This approach isn't going to stick because John needs to come to this conclusion himself, otherwise he's not going to believe it.

I asked, "How do you show John that the devil you know is better than the one you don't?" The MD responded, "I could show him an alternative option, one that wouldn't align with our culture."

And there it is!

This tactic worked because the MD was able to get John to imagine an alternative whereby they merge with a huge corporate conglomerate, and John could see he'd just become another number with no real autonomy or independence. Imagining such an unwanted scenario showed him that the merger on the table actually looked very attractive.

What Did You Notice?

1. The problem was not diagnosed correctly, because no one considered John's character traits, motives, or feelings.

2. Until John's perspective was acknowledged and understood, the MD was not able to influence him.

3. John would have been triggered and become defensive if the MD had pushed his agenda without knowing the real problem.

4. When people are triggered, you are unable to influence. GAME OVER.

In my work, it's safe to say that most executives are empathetic at a surface level; they're unable to truly dig deep into how others are feeling. There are many levels of empathy and the surface level is pretty void of any real impact. It's level one empathy, where you can hear someone, but you're void of any real understanding of what they're saying.

The second level is where the magic happens. It's where you hear what the person is saying, but you also understand their perspective. Again, you don't need to agree with them, but you can understand them. This level offers connection and provides a deeper level of context for more effective communication.

At level three, you can hear the person, understand their perspective, and feel what it's like to view things from their perspective. At this level, the connection is at its healthiest. You're reading the other person, watching for body language cues, decoding what's being said, and evaluating what's not being said. You can interpret what you're seeing and hearing. This deep level of connection is where you can feel empathy and genuine understanding. John's story is an example of the process of going deep to understand another person's perspective, feel how they're feeling, and truly submerge yourself and step into their shoes.

Empathy and influence serve as opportunities for problem solving, and I've always believed that problems present enormous opportunities for growth. But the trouble is that many people, employee or C-suite executive, don't know what they don't know. This highly effective influencing skill, that goes beyond the surface level evades them, so they never submerge themselves in the profound experience of a problem.

Our brains don't make it easy for us, considering we're wired to opt for the path of least resistance in order to survive. Unless you're pushing beyond your default behaviour, you won't be developing the deep empathy necessary to serve in a leadership capacity. Empathy is not a nice-to-have; it's a non-negotiable in the leadership of tomorrow. Are you future fit?

Tough Empathy

There is one more form of empathy which is not discussed as much as the others: tough empathy. This is a critical element of effective leadership. You can only leverage tough empathy once you've mastered the fundamental traits of empathy.

In leadership, empathy alone is not enough. Tough empathy is where the magic happens.

Example - Paul

A leader Paul discussed with me the challenges he was having with an employee. Paul talked about the ongoing support he continued to provide because he wanted to ensure he was setting the person up for success. He had tried various strategies, such as one on one training, coaching, setting specific improvement goals with clear timelines and extended training such as partnering the employee up with other team members. The team spent six months attempting to support this person, but there was no improvement.

Reports from client's about receiving incorrect information, complaints about the employee's lack of response, tasks incomplete or lacked attention to detail continued despite everyone's support efforts.

I could see the employee didn't have the right attitude to grow, and Paul didn't want to make the tough decision about letting him go.

My job in this instance was to ask Paul enough questions to lead him to his conclusion. Why was he holding onto the employee? What was the cost to the team, in terms of lack of support, and using their time repeatedly training? Why was the decision difficult? What was the next step?

Paul realised he couldn't let the situation go on any longer because he had a responsibility to the broader team. He realised that no matter how understanding the entire team was, they were resentful of the lagging co-worker because they've picked up the slack for too long.

Paul reflected on the situation and realised that his hesitation in taking action was because he was second-guessing himself, that he'd not done enough or he hadn't seen the signs of where the issues lay. By keeping the employee on, he was impacting the team. Plus, the employee's confidence was diminishing as each day passed.

Taking a tough and empathetic approach is about bearing in mind not only what the person wants, but most importantly what the person needs.

A leader uses tough empathy when they commit to their team members, by saying, "I won't back away. I will support you, but I will also challenge you to level up and become the best version of yourself."

How can a leader express a sincere, compassionate, empathetic understanding towards a team member, all while being tough and challenging them? Is this not contradictory? Quite the opposite. If a team member has a problem and a leader shows compassion towards that employee, it's also an opportunity for the employee to take ownership and become accountable for solving that problem. The 'tough' aspect helps people take ownership for the problem and find the solution themselves.

The paradox of tough empathy resolves when a leader is tough on the outcome/problem but shows compassion combined with owning their responsibility for the person.

Example – Parenting

I remember watching on as my husband taught our son, Ethan, to ride his bike. My son would fall off and lose confidence, and he begged my husband to not let go of him. My husband had empathy for our son, but he didn't run alongside holding the bike up day after day, so that Ethan wouldn't fall again. Ethan may have wanted him to do that, but it's not what he needed.

My husband showed empathy; he put himself in our child's shoes to understand what he was feeling. He used compassion to persuade Ethan to get back on the bike because it was the only way he was going to learn to ride.

This is an example of tough empathy in action.

Tough empathy goes beyond showing compassion. Tough empathy steps into the other persons shoes, appreciates how they might be feeling, and evaluates what they need versus what they want.

Tough Empathy in Practice

I've witnessed many managers go for interpersonal skills training, return knowing they need to improve their empathy towards others... and still not know how.

Some people are natural leaders. They don't need to be trained to care about their employees. They naturally empathise with the people they lead, understanding that they're only as good as the people around them, so they invest most of their time in setting their team up for success.

Example – Tough Choices

I led a business through the global financial crisis, which coincided with the disruption of the industry we operated in. Our competitors were closing their doors around us, as they were unable to remain solvent.

I needed to make some tough decisions about redundancies within the business. These were not easy decisions but nonetheless they needed to be made.

Rather than sending our HR director or the department heads to deliver the news to each person, I flew to each state over two days and personally delivered the message, explaining why and how we reached the decision.

I remember one young lady in Perth called Sara. She'd only been with the company a year, straight out of university, and she was full of so much enthusiasm. When I delivered the news to Sara, she was very understanding and she said to me, "I hope I didn't let you down. It's been an honour to have you as a mentor, and in this short time you've taught me so much."

I'm sure you can imagine how this made me feel. I felt like the worst person in the world! Yet, it didn't change the necessity of the decision. While I cared for Sara and was deeply empathic to how difficult this was for her, I had no choice if I wanted to make the best decisions for the greater good of the business, to remain commercially viable, and protect the other employees. It was a tough time, but the decisions were critical.

Understanding and practicing tough empathy can be complicated. It is the challenge of managing a situation, considering the people within it, and making tough decisions. These tough decisions can still be made in a kind way.

Example – Underperforming

While working within a client's business, there was a situation whereby the team leaders of a call centre had a new employee who was consistently making mistakes and underperforming. The team leaders were trying everything they could to help the employee, offering ongoing training and supporting him by answering all his questions. However, no matter how much time and resources they invested in him, nothing improved. Each time we met they would come up with alternative training strategies; it was time to draw a line in the sand.

I asked them if they believed he could improve. They both agreed that no, it didn't seem likely. When asked what they needed to do, they both said they wanted to keep trying, and reasoned, "We feel sorry for him. He has a family to support."

To cut a long story short, they didn't want to step out of their comfort zones and make the call. I helped them do just that by encouraging them to consider the implications of keeping him, including the impact it was having on the broader team. This situation could have gone on and on, but as leaders they had a responsibility to their team to make tough calls when required.

Pushing people beyond their comfort zones is my responsibility and the responsibility of all leaders because we make a commitment to serve others when working with them. I made a promise that my people would learn and grow.

Tough empathy involves finding a balance between honouring the best decision for the greater good while respecting the needs of individuals. Balancing the two is not an easy task. Great leaders know when to give, when to pull back, and when to push people beyond their comfort zones. At its core, tough empathy is an approach for solving problems and raising the performance bar for leaders and teams.

Empathy and growth have a level of interdependence. As a leader, you best serve all your stakeholders by recognising this fact.

Empathy and Relevance

For businesses to remain relevant in this fast-paced ever-evolving market, leaders must put people at the heart of everything that they do. One fundamental element of any business is to serve and improve the lives of your clients and your employees.

If you don't help your team to immerse themselves in the sensory experience of your customer, to put themselves into the customer's shoes, and to show compassion for their problem, then you can't develop, let alone deploy, a solution for them.

So, how do you remain relevant? When we talk about adaptability in future chapters, you'll see how empathy connects with many facets of business, not just to leadership.

Master Non-verbal Cues

There's a renowned study on communication, conducted by Albert Mehrabian (2011) of UCLA, which concluded that there are three elements in any face-to-face communication: words, tone of voice and non-verbal cues.

- **?** Words account for 7 per cent of our communication.

- **?** Tone of voice accounts for 38 per cent.

- **?** Body language accounts for 55 per cent.

For example, when someone verbally communicates, "I'm happy in my work!" while displaying a defensive body language and avoiding eye-contact, it becomes evident that the person is not communicating honestly. According to Mehrabian's findings, our instinct is to trust the non-verbal communication rather than the words used.

It's essential, then, to master and understand how we are interpreting what others are saying to us beyond their words. Here are some points you need to consider about your communication skills:

- **?** Is ego clouding your judgement?

- **?** Are you too comfortable?

- **?** Are you using your active listening skills to hear beyond the surface level? Pay attention to tone of voice and body language. Factor in people's emotional triggers, their perspective and motives, and deep dive into understanding the context of their communication.

- **?** Are you rushing to give advice? Think things over. Better still, help the other person to develop their thinking and conclude for themselves.

- **?** Do you dismiss people's concerns offhand or interrupt others because you think they're incorrect?

- **?** Do you change the subject when you're not interested in having the conversation?

? Do you allow people time to articulate themselves? Ask questions to develop your understanding of their perspective.

? Can you read non-verbal behaviour?

? How do you praise and recognise your team? Pay attention to people's actions or achievements and remember what it is you want to encourage. When you give praise, ensure your words are genuine.

? Are you able to give people your undivided attention? Don't look at your phone, check your emails, or take phone calls when a person wants to talk to you. How would you feel if someone did that to you?

? Putting yourself in another person's shoes can be difficult. When working with clients who need to see from their employee's perspective, I ask them to envisage the same situation, but between them and their boss.

? Do you take the time to encourage people, particularly those who don't often speak up in meetings? It's as simple as asking them what they think, or questions that stimulate contribution and help to boost confidence.

Exercise - Open Questions

Small steps can create significant change. Challenge yourself to ask five open questions the next time you're listening to someone before you say anything about yourself, the issue or, the circumstance.

___

CHAPTER SEVEN

Mastering Influence and Persuasion – Become an Unstoppable Leader of Influence

When I say 'influential people', Richard Branson, Steve Jobs, and Oprah probably spring to mind. They seem to have a skill which we lesser mortals lack. They are high achievers with grand vision and hordes of followers, and they know how to create empowered accountable teams. They inspire the kind of loyalty most of us dream of, and they do it using a specific set of skills which can be learnt. That's right, influence and persuasion are skills and you can develop them, too.

These are skills which work together; two sides of the same coin. That might surprise you if you see persuasion in terms of marketing or sleazy salespeople. Great leaders know persuasion isn't about talking people into things or forcing decisions. Instead, it's a form of influence.

Your role as leader is to gather your people, along with their values, experiences, and desires, and lead them as a united team to achieve group and organisational goals. You're not going to manage that by issuing orders.

What Is Influence, and How Do You Master It?

Before we can master influence, we must understand what it is not:

- It's not manipulation.

- It's not forcefulness.

- It's not getting your own way.

It is a leadership skill, a framework. It's the ability to trigger a thought within the mind of an individual that encourages and prompts them to an actionable conclusion.

It's a leadership fundamental which involves encouraging people to follow a set example, or leading them to the desired outcome, one that they've concluded themselves. Ultimately, we're trying to influence someone's behaviour.

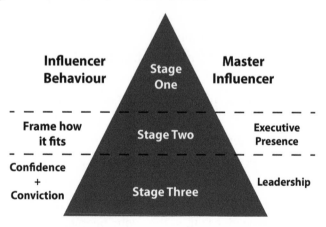

When we seek to become a master influencer, there are three stages of mastery.

Stage One – You're a leader who operates with confidence and conviction.

Stage Two – You're a leader who operates with executive presence, and you frame how the situation fits from the other person's perspective. As outlined with John's example earlier:

- You consider the desired outcome, and you are powerfully persuading, strategically steering, and inspiring commitment.

- You consider human behaviour, and you diagnose the obstacles, by considering character traits, motives, and feelings.

- You're empathetic, and you seek to understand the other person's perspective. You don't have to agree with their viewpoint, but attempt to find their truth. No one person owns the truth; we all own a piece of it.

Stage Three - You inspire commitment, and you've mastered influencing, by using empathy to understand what the barriers are that stop people from taking action. Barriers that stop people from owning their accountability, and help enable people to break through limitations, fears, and concerns so that they can move themselves to conclusions and actions.

Remember

- To master the art of influence, you must come from a place of genuine interest in understanding or supporting others; not a place of pure self-interest.

- If there is any hesitation or doubt in your communication, people will sense it, and the hesitation or doubt will be the perspective that dominates.

- Managing the frame is about how others are perceiving the situation. John's story is an example of the process of going deep to understand another person's perspective, feel how they're feeling, and truly submerge yourself and step into their shoes.

- Ultimately, you create a perception which influences behaviour and provides a win-win situation.

Influence Doesn't Come with Your Position

It doesn't matter how powerful your role; it doesn't equal influence. The ability to dictate is power; the ability to guide thoughts and actions is influence. People may follow your instructions, but it won't create change in them. Power and influence are different forms of leadership. Power leaders suck their teams dry of happiness and motivation, and have a high turnover of staff. Influential leaders build relationships and trust with their people who are then willing to grow, take risks, and stay engaged with their work.

How the Brain Reacts to Power and Influence

The brain is a complicated structure, but essentially, different sections are responsible for different human responses.

The Lizard Brain

The lizard brain, sometimes called the reptilian brain, is the primitive part of our brain which is primarily concerned with keeping us alive and safe. It's where our survival instinct springs from. The lizard brain includes the amygdala, a core part of the limbic system where our emotions are processed. So, here we have a brain which concentrates on keeping us alive and manages emotions like fear and worry, along with memories of past (often traumatic) experiences. You can imagine the control this brain has over the way you see things like change and how you respond to it. It is primal!

Initially, the lizard brain is likely to respond to power leaders purely as a survival tactic. Do as you're told or else! Stephen Pressfield calls this brain the "Resistance" and says it's a way of thinking which keeps us small and unnoticeable. It puts limits on the areas of the brain available to you so it can control your response. You resist your urge to speak up, try something new, or rebel. You procrastinate because doing nothing is often safer than doing something, and you never complete anything because you don't want to be judged. After all, who would want to stand out when there's a power-infused boss spreading orders around?

A power leader will only ever produce a team which runs on fear and anonymity, which will tire quickly and never reach high performance.

The Executive Brain

The leader who uses influence instead of power triggers an entirely different type of mindset called the executive brain. The executive brain includes the prefrontal cortex, which is involved with logic, reasoning, problem solving, creativity, and decision making. It helps manage your memory, and the organisation and regulation of your thoughts and behaviours. It works with high-level consciousness, visualisation, imagination, and goal seeking.

This brain has some control over the lizard brain. For example, you may find yourself in a situation where you feel afraid and want to run away, but the executive brain overrules instinct by recognising that you can't run fast enough. It seeks and presents a better solution. The executive brain can pull you out of the survival mode your lizard brain put you into, and help you function more effectively.

Leaders who use influence and persuasion with their teams are working with this high-level part of the brain. They tap into our need to belong and contribute, as well as our need to have a purpose. Using the executive brain helps us to overcome resistance to change, quieting the lizard by offering the security of support and encouragement and a vision of a compelling potential future.

The result is a motivated team who knows where they are going and why, is committed to getting there, and is willing to find the best way to do it; a team which is highly engaged with their work and loyal to the person who helped them grow.

It's evident that for long-term results, influence defeats power. Mastering influence can help you excel in leadership roles and encourage people to follow you willingly.

How to Develop Greater Influence

Through years of helping clients strengthen their leadership skills, I've found three key components vital to developing influence:

1. Powerful persuasion

2. Tactical leadership

3. Passionate action

As we move on through the book, we'll take a closer look at each component and how it contributes to your desired outcome.

Powerful Persuasion

Leaders who want to influence through persuasion need to find the motives of the people they lead.

- What is important to them?

- What do they want?

- What are their goals?

- What are their triggers?

- What are the beliefs they already hold about themselves, you, their work, and the world around them which influence their actions?

You're looking for some common ground and the only way to find it is by establishing an honest and open connection. It's all reliant on their trust in you. Every leadership action is reliant on trust; you in the team and the team in you. Unless you have established a solid relationship with your people, they won't trust you enough to be persuaded.

We don't operate purely on logic; we're emotional and social creatures, whether we admit it or not. Using empathy, you can establish common ground with another person by finding shared experiences or values. When you find that space, you can start to explore their perspective and begin to understand how you can encourage their growth.

At some stage, you're likely to encounter their lizard brain, and they'll start throwing up excuses for their inaction. You've encountered an emotion which has triggered a fight-or-flight response. At this point, you may keep on with your conversation, but you'll probably be seen as an adversary rather than a caring leader.

Triggers

We all have triggers. They're a result of a negative association with a place, person, or event. Triggers are emotional reactions to something which has happened in the past. When you encounter a situation that hurts you or causes you to fail, you don't want to go through it again. While you may not be aware of it, this emotion remains in your subconscious and will be triggered again when you are in a similar situation. You might be as surprised as anyone else when it rears its ugly head, or you might not even realise you've been triggered.

I was once facilitating a group workshop in New Zealand for an executive team from all around the country. The training consisted of fifteen people. During the session, two individuals sat with their arms crossed, and when I attempted to engage with them, they were despondent and closed-minded.

The objective and training outcomes were for the executive team to become more self- aware of how they were holding themselves (and therefore their organisation) back from higher levels of performance.

I taught the executives the principles in this book, but I was also tasked with ensuring these leaders stepped out of their comfort zones.

One of the resistant individuals, Amanda, wanted to continue to shift blame to others for how she was feeling. Amanda was struggling to take responsibility for her feelings or her role in creating situations and she was holding grudges.

Amanda told the story of a time when she was asked to speak at an internal conference the organisation held, she had only been allocated 15 minutes to speak. In her mind, the person organising the conference did not respect or value her expertise. She was triggered by not feeling valued.

Amanda was triggered just telling the story because she believed she was treated unfairly. In this instance, Amanda was letting her ego hold her back. If something happens to threaten the image we have of ourselves, our ego rises, but most people don't recognise this.

When Amanda is triggered, her brain thinks she's experiencing an immediate threat. As a result, she becomes defensive, and her language and tone become aggressive and argumentative. In turn, people respond by backing down or away from Amanda when she's behaving like this. She's learnt that by acting like this, no one challenges her and she gets her way.

In this instance, I used empathy to connect with Amanda. I said, "I can only imagine how that would have made you feel", because she felt undervalued and disrespected. From there, I asked Amanda to consider another perspective apart from her current one-dimensional one. She became agitated again. She didn't like to be challenged as she was used to people backing away, but having people retreat from her when she behaved in this manner was not serving anyone.

Her response was that there was no other perspective, and she wanted to change the subject. Well, that wasn't going to happen because I knew that this evasion wouldn't serve Amanda.

I said, "Amanda, I get the feeling you're uncomfortable with this conversation. Can you tell me why this might be the case?" To which she responded, "I don't want to talk about it now as I need time to reflect on a different perspective."

I agreed with Amanda that reflection time would help her, and I asked when might be a suitable time to continue the discussion. We decided to regroup a few days later and the resulting conversation was very productive.

I didn't let the conversation go without a timeline to pursue it further, because the ability to see a varied perspective was critical for Amanda's growth. Asking her for a timeline to conclude the discussion was a way of holding her accountable for doing the work.

What did you notice?

- Amanda's triggers were noticeable to everyone but herself.

- Amanda had limited self-awareness in this instance.

- Acknowledging and showing empathy towards Amanda's perspectives allowed me to disarm her as opposed to triggering her more. This was genuine empathy.

- I didn't let Amanda's defensive and hostile behaviour deter me from pursuing a potentially uncomfortable conversation.

- Amanda responded in a defensive and hostile manner because this was her programmed behaviour, which usually resulted in others retreating from the awkward conversations.

Influence and Triggers

Thanks to the years of work that I've done, I'm now fully aware when I'm triggered. It doesn't mean that I'm immune to triggers; I've just learned to become aware when it's happening and can choose how I respond as a result. I'm also able to identify when others are triggered and I can prepare for conversations considering what I know about people's characters and what might trigger them.

When influencing, you must come from a place of genuine interest in wanting to support or help others work through what might be holding them back. True influence should not be used to manipulate people. If you attempt to use it that way, people will eventually see right through the tactic.

Even in a positive conversation, perhaps you're working with a team member and influencing them towards change, it's quite likely you'll encounter a trigger. This is a lizard brain response. How do you handle it?

First, learn to spot the precursory warning signs. Leaders with high EQ might notice physical changes in the person they're talking to, such as a flushed complexion or tightened posture. It might show in the way the person is speaking: no answers, disengaged, making excuses, sarcasm, rejecting your suggestions, or even outright anger.

You need to understand the trigger. Asking, "Are you okay?" may help the person recognise what's happening and control their reaction. It's a great way to encourage someone to talk. Other gentle questions that may help to uncover a trigger are:

- **(?)** I have the feeling something about this is making you uncomfortable, would you like to talk about it?

- **(?)** Have I said or done something here which bothers you?

Remember, the person's reaction is not directed at you; it's a response to something in their past. Sometimes the best course of action is to take a break and let the person have a breather. Invite the person to join you for coffee. A change of scenery and mindset may help.

Disarming Triggers

The best way to disarm a trigger is to take the emotion out of it, but that doesn't mean ignoring it.

- Acknowledge the person's emotion and cognitively empathise with how they feel. Be genuine about it because the pain is real to them.

- Ask them what has made them feel this way. Encourage them to tell you their story. Let them get it all out.

- Listen for cues behind their response such as fear of change, failing at a new challenge, lack of skill, or worry about leaving a team. If you can identify the fear, you can deal with it.

- Thank the person for telling you their story. It takes guts, and they've honoured you by sharing it. Thank them and move the conversation towards solutions by saying something like, "I understand why you feel this way so let's see how together we can get a happier result this time."

- Summarise what you heard. In a few short sentences, describe the situation they were in, the issue that arose, and how it's made them feel. Always end by asking, "Is that right?"

- Check for emotion again and ask for a commitment to move on; "So, if we can find a way to do (the change/ situation) without (the issue), how would you feel about that?"

When you talk the situation through in this way, you're working with the person's executive brain, calling on their ability to clarify their feelings and think rationally about them.

With focus, preparation, and ongoing execution (practice) you'll be able to master this technique and use it without thinking. Focused work is what makes it work.

Example – Jess

The primary stakeholder, the MD, James - he was a little bit of a control freak, as many business owners are because their business is their baby. Therefore, if we consider James' character type Jess knew that he was a little reluctant to let go. Jess understood this concern, and we talked about how the idea to promote Jess, needed to come from James. Jess also knew that it would be hard for James to relinquish responsibility because people who have control freak tendencies are usually perfectionists who feel vulnerable to anything outside of their control.

Jess also knew that a critical driver for James was to expand the business globally and that he would be unable to do so if he continued to manage the day to day operation.

Jess understood James fundamental values too, which were honesty and strong family values. James owned the business with his brother, and Jess knew the brother was pushing for James to let go.

Jess offered to support James with a few tasks, to relieve his busy schedule, and she became a valuable contributor to the team's growth. She did this in a very subtle way, and she assumed the next level role organically, without asking for permission to contribute to support the team to grow.

Jess became a valuable asset to the business, and she proved her worth, as a result James and his brother offered

Jess the General Manager role and a considerable pay rise. Jess knew that if she demonstrated her worth and built trust with James and his brother, they'd have no choice but to promote her.

This technique allowed her to influence without threatening anyone and persuaded others towards the desired outcome. The stakeholders soon became her collaborators in accomplishing an outcome, a promotion.

Now you understand how the brain works, how to manage the lizard brain and influence the executive brain. You know the three components of influence, why they're essential, and how to use them to inspire action. You have everything you need to help you become an unstoppable leader of influence. In the next chapter, we'll discover how to harness questions to create high-performing teams that are taking passionate action towards their goals.

CHAPTER EIGHT

Empowering and Sustaining High-performance Teams

Everyone's Perception (Brain) Is Different

A human brain is a machine with vast wiring, and it functions by finding connections, associations, and links between different pieces of information. Our experiences, memories, skills, and traits are a broad set of complex wiring or neural pathways.

Just as physical exercise builds your muscles, the neural pathways in your brain grow with mental exercise (learning), and the neurons develop greater connectivity. This is called neuroplasticity.

Neuroplasticity provides us with the most significant opportunity as humans: we can rewire our brains by thinking. Think about it this way. You and I purchased a computer together, the same model on the same day from the same customer service representative at the same retailer, and we both went off and used the computer for a year.

A year later, my computer no longer functions and I ask you if I can use your computer. You graciously agree. I start using it and I try to find all the information I need, but it's difficult because you've set up your folders and organised your documents in different places. You haven't set up your computer like I set up mine. Think of our brains' wiring as the same. Our experiences, memories, skills, and traits define how our brain is wired, and our brains are all wired differently.

Consider what happens when you tell someone what they need to do. Are they able to process information in the same way you do? No, because their wiring is different from yours. They have a unique perspective because of their unique wiring. Therefore, the fastest way to transform people's performance is by helping them to think for themselves, and to find solutions themselves. When people think for themselves, their brain is finding the necessary connectors to form new neural pathways. These pathways are made based on the information already stored and the new information we seek to download and store.

In order to lead a person to reach the goal you set for them, you must guide them with their own thinking. Once you've mastered this skill, you'll transform your people into high performers, who are delivering on goals and exceeding expectations time and time again. The added bonus here is that when we create new neural pathways—ideas—we're motivated and excited to act.

Creating high-performing teams starts with helping others to improve their thinking. This is the best place to improve performance and hold people accountable. As a leader, you have a responsibility to set people up for success and to help them develop because of your presence, by building accountability.

Tactical Leadership

If you want to lead your team in a different direction, the best way is to guide their thinking so they see the same goals you do and map their own route to them. Now, this isn't always a straightforward process because you need to speak to their emotions before you can connect with their logic. How do you do that? You talk about the consequences of not making the change. You hit the pain points, knowing people will do almost anything to avoid the pain. When you help people to think for themselves, you're creating a strong motivation for action.

Dictating instructions, or the appearance thereof, can make people resistant to change. Our role as leader is about helping people to make their own connections and create new neural pathways. Therefore, tactical leadership means helping people to identify for themselves what the problem is, what they want to change, and the best course of action. You do this with carefully planned questions such as:

- **?** This is how I see the problem/situation; is this how you see it too?

- **?** How does this make you feel?

- **?** What are the consequences of this situation?

- **?** How would you like to feel?

- **?** How could we fix this?

- **?** What would you like to see happen?

- **?** What are our alternatives for making that happen?

- **?** Which of these solutions will best meet your needs?

Through this process, you have established the framework for your case, helped the team find the evidence to support it, and tuned into their emotions. This shifts their mindset from resistance to the desired change. You aren't dominating. Your questions are strategically leading the team towards an outcome which works for all of you. You are empowering people to make their own choices.

It's a process you facilitate rather than dictate, and by empowering your people to make their own choices, you create team ownership of, and commitment to, the outcomes.

If you want to influence others, or establish your seniority and exhibit more authority, then you need to start asking more questions. The person asking the questions is in control of the destination and leading the discussion to the desired outcome. It's almost impossible to make a mistake asking questions.

Here's how to influence people with questions and to dominate any meeting.

- You may have heard the expression - preparation accounts for 90 per cent of success. I've had a front row seat to the truth of this phrase. So, prepare your questions in advance. Brainstorm your desired outcome and the questions you need to ask to lead the discussion down the path to the desired result.

- Consider the varied directions the discussion might head and prepare a list of questions for each. Consider what questions you could ask if the discussion heads in the wrong direction, so you can bring it back on track.

- Make sure you have a genuine intent with your desired outcomes.

❐ Always ask your questions with an open mind that seeks to understand. Use a calm and friendly tone of voice, otherwise your meeting or approach could be perceived as an interrogation.

On a side note, one of the tips I give leaders who are unsure of speaking up in meetings or need some breathing space to think is to use some general prompts, such as:

? That's interesting. Can you tell me more?

? Why do you think that?

? How do you know that?

? What does the data tell you about that?

? Can you go more in depth with that thought?

? Tell us more about your level of confidence with regards to the outcome?

? What are the risks?

? How could we fix this?

? What would you like to see happen?

? What's your next move?

One of the best tools you can have as a leader is a series of questions that you've memorised to use in any conversation to influence others. Questions allow you to get people to open up and to understand what they are thinking. They also help to build trust and to set people up for success.

Commit a few questions to memory and use them in interactions moving forward. The more you ask questions, the more this will become your foundation for improving people's performance, holding people accountable, and creating high-performing teams and organisations.

Your Secret Weapon – Awkward Silence

Influencing others by leading them down a path to a desired conclusion is one of the most effective techniques for holding people accountable. But when using questioning techniques, the biggest and most common mistake made is not waiting for a response after posing a question. Most people follow the question up with further explanation and it loses its power. People struggle to sit comfortably in the 'awkward silence'. Watch for it when you observe people asking questions and you'll notice it immediately. When you're using questioning techniques, wait for an answer. This is a powerful move on your part. Become comfortable with the silence.

Passionate Action

Tactical leadership encourages commitment to group decisions from individuals because each member has contributed to them. But commitment won't last without help. It slips away in the face of challenge. The passion wears off over time and disappears when people feel as though they're working alone. Without passion, there's no action.

As a leader, you can keep your team inspired and sustain their passion for generating action. To do that, you need to inspire their commitment to you as a leader and as an individual.

This is important because relationships and trust always precede good work, even if we don't realise it. When you think about how well you work for someone you like compared with someone you don't, you'll notice a different feeling, energy, and outcome. The experience and the work you produce is always better when you work with someone to whom you have loyalty and commitment.

The leader who inspires commitment builds personal connections with the people they work with. Simon Sinek says, "People don't buy what you do; they buy why you do it. And what you do simply proves what you believe." Sharing your passion and talking positively about the work involved will create a solid basis for creating an honest and open relationship. It's also motivating to know you're working towards a common goal.

People will respond to you as a leader if you're seeking to understand their perspective and supporting them to be the best versions of themselves, as opposed to managing through the command-and-control technique.

Work together, talk together, solve problems together, and assess your progress together. Do what you need to do to increase the unity of your team and strengthen their sense of ownership. Praise good work, respect contributions, and allow the team to manage itself under your guidance. Let your passion keep their passion burning.

What about accountability? People are naturally motivated to live up to their commitments. Most of us have an inner driver which keeps us accountable, and we respond better to it than we do to directions from our so-called superiors. We also instinctively hold ourselves responsible when we've committed to someone who has put their faith in us. This is where the passion for sustained action comes from.

Accountability and Measuring Performance

What gets measured improves. You'll never have success without focus and measure. Setting key performance indicators, targets, and/or critical success factors is critical to high performance. How you set these will vary between businesses, however, once identified, these metrics should be linked to your strategy and then broken down into bite-size pieces for each division and role.

I always use benchmark data to assess and review performance. A few years ago, I started working with a client who had no data on his business performance. When we implemented this strategy, along with the other strategies in this book, his business grew 38 per cent in the first year, and 68 per cent (more than $5 million) in the second. The growth came by measuring and improving performance, creating a high-performing team. There were no added expenses in this process, meaning his profit soared by 245 per cent. Now that's not a bad outcome; it's one that many business owners or leaders would welcome.

Now you know how the brain functions and why providing your team with answers to their problems is ineffective in improving performance. I can categorically confirm that any short-term gain will evolve into a long-term cost and an opportunity lost for improved performance. By taking the command-and-control approach, you hinder the development of individuals and rob yourself of fresh ideas. Many heads are better than one. When you choose not to influence or develop others, you hamstring yourself. As a leader, you have a responsibility to others to improve their thinking and set them up for success, helping them become the best versions of themselves. Now you know how to use the components of influence, inspire action, and create accountable high-performing teams. You can now start using these techniques to lead your team towards your vision.

PART III

LEADING BUSINESS

———

CHAPTER NINE

Adaptability Quotient – Your Silver Bullet to Innovation and Remaining Relevant

You've heard of IQ and EQ but have you heard of AQ, the adaptability quotient? It's becoming another 'must have' for career success. Adaptability quotient has been recognised as "the future of work" by Fast Company magazine. But why is it so important? And what is it?

Adaptability is a required trait in both workers and leaders as it helps companies keep up with the rapidly changing trends that are radically reshaping business and the modern workplace. It's a skill that enables you to quickly learn new behaviours and skills, and change strategy in response to changing circumstances. If 2020 has taught us anything, it's the importance of adapting to survive. I've spruiked the importance of adaptability for many years now but until COVID19, numerous leaders and organisations hadn't appreciated the risk of dismissing it.

A PwC study, *Adapt to Survive*, says, "Businesses need the ability to adapt to meet these emerging opportunities. And that requires adaptable people, many of whom are not in the right roles, the organisation or even in the same industry—yet."

Your AQ matters more than any other metric when disruption surrounds you; when the pressure is on and the stakes are high. So, are you ready? Is your team ready? Is your organisation ready? How will you choose to adapt your leadership?

A UK study by Right Management surveyed HR decision makers in over a thousand organisations. Of those surveyed, 91 per cent said that the ability to cope with change and uncertainty was likely to be a prime reason for their selection of future employees and leaders. The same report found that 98 per cent of organisations have experienced major organisational change over the past five years. This trend will only increase.

Adaptability Wins

Today's workplace has evolved into a fast-paced environment of constant change, and relies on technology and innovation to enhance and streamline systems, as a basis for cost saving and to achieve global reach.

Somewhere amongst the technology and innovation are the people. During this technological revolution, the needs of people are often forgotten. The companies that will survive are those that adapt to the innovation-driven world of change. But technology doesn't innovate; people do. So, the surviving companies will also be the ones that look after their people.

This puts a lot of pressure on you as a leader. You'll need to call on your people skills as well as your adaptability. In fact, adaptability has been described as the "new competitive advantage" by the Harvard Business Review. Today's leaders are having to find ways to succeed in rapid and radically changing market conditions, including embracing new business models and more forward-thinking ways of working and leading.

As with any other characteristic, the ability to adapt varies from person to person. When it comes to the survival of the business and the individual, it's those with high AQ who will lead the way.

Businesses that can't or don't adapt will fail. Think of Kodak or BlackBerry; their low AQ meant they couldn't recognise or respond to changes in technology or demand. Not only do these failed giants have quite a lot in common, but their stories merge into a single powerful parallel about the dangers of success and the consequent failure to adapt, innovate, and ultimately remain relevant.

How Adaptable Are You?

You might find that a hard question to answer so let me break it down further.

- How open are you to accepting suggestions from others once your suggestion has been outvoted?

- How do you react when something unexpected happens at work or at home?

- When there's a need to step out of your comfort zone to get a job done, how do you respond?

- How easily do you fall into the mode of idea generation?

- How well do you manage your emotions during times of change so you can stay focused?

? How confident are you that you are likely to generate new solutions to challenges as they arise?

? How confident are you that you can adapt to survive and thrive?

The Keys to Adaptability

In their book, *The Oz Principle*, Roger Connors and Tom Smith list four key steps which help you to apply and increase your AQ. They are:

1. **See it.** See the problem, acknowledge it, and understand the pressure to change.

2. **Own it.** Take ownership of the problem and the results.

3. **Solve it.** Find a solution by looking at what can be done differently.

4. **Do it.** Implement said solution and follow through.

The starting point for adapting to change is taking control of the situation instead of being controlled by it. At its heart is the recognition that things have to change and that you're the leader who pioneers a new way forward. Pioneers are game changers. They see things differently, looking at problems and challenges from different angles in their quest to find a solution. They think differently, coming up with new and original ideas or, at the very least, harnessing the creative power of their teams to forge solutions.

The great leaders of tomorrow will be those who are able to nurture adaptable teams towards innovation and creativity. Perhaps surprisingly, this may not be as difficult as it sounds because when you look after your teams and their environment, creativity flourishes.

Creativity and Innovation

I think it's important to distinguish between the two terms because many of us are uncomfortable with the concept of creativity and we worry that we don't have what it takes to be creative. In simple terms, creativity is a freedom of mind and imagination. It can also be about problem solving, and it certainly not something exclusively for the artsy crowd.

Innovation is about taking these new ideas and solutions and making them tangible, making them happen. It's about implementation. Without creativity, there will be nothing new to implement. Without innovation, great creative ideas would never get implemented!

Matching the Quality of Innovation and the Quality of People Skills

From a business point of view, innovation is more measurable than creativity. This leads to the problem of managers pushing for ideas without creating an environment where creativity can flourish. Executive leadership reverses that process, creating an atmosphere which encourages people to create and share new ideas. Creativity and innovation need to come from the top. Even if you don't consider yourself particularly creative, you can increase your level of creativity and you can nurture it in others. Creativity begins with self-leadership.

Leading Others Towards Creativity and Innovation

Today's workplace is heavy with technology. Often, people spend whole days alone, staring at a computer screen or device of some kind. Technology is great but it does tend to isolate people from each other. The result is people who are socially and emotionally separated. Considering humans are wired to be social, there's a huge gap here which needs to be filled. It's hard to be creative when the only input you have is from a screen. It's hard to be adaptable when you see nothing beyond your device.

To build innovation and creativity in your team and spark it in individual members, you need to change the way they are working. You need to change the way they are thinking and feeling about work, too. This is about redefining roles, boundaries, and the work environment. Creativity will thrive if you let it, but it must come from the top.

Even if *you* have the big ideas, you need a clever, creative team to actualise them. But what if you don't have the big ideas? What if you believe you're not innovative or creative? Jeffrey Baumgartner, author of *The Way of the Innovation Master*, says this:

"An innovative leader does not even need to be the person who creates the idea behind an innovation. Often, she simply recognises a great idea – perhaps devised by a subordinate – and envisions the path that leads to that idea becoming a reality. Indeed, I would argue that creative genius is less important in an innovative leader than is the ability to form a vision around an idea or set of ideas. And once she has formed that vision, she needs to be able to share with employees, suppliers and business partners the vision as well as enthusiasm for turning that vision into a reality."

As a leader, you have the influence and the ability to empower your people to be brave enough to think differently about the way you do things. It's your role to make creativity and innovation a normal way of working. You'll read in the next couple of chapters how innovation generally starts with solving a problem.

Techniques for Leading Others Towards Innovation

1. **Be a role model.** Trust yourself enough to trust others. Model the behaviours you want to see, such as openness, honesty, questioning the norm, taking risks, and accepting failure (but learning from it). You can't ask your team to do something you wouldn't. As a leader with influence and authority, you set the standard others will aspire to. Make sure you're modelling the standards you expect from your team.

2. **Empower your team to act.** It's no good expecting people to think outside the box if they don't have the power to do it. Change the rules if you must. You're changing the culture, after all. Talk to your people and be clear about their boundaries. Let them stretch. Give them permission to go for it. Encourage adaptability as a character trait and respect it in them even when it challenges your own thought processes.

3. **Let them be hands-on.** If you want them to solve a problem, ensure they have all the information they need, even if it means getting them to experience the problem for themselves. They will have a better idea of the whole process as well as the impact it has on the business. You can't be truly creative at a distance.

4. **Foster the attitude that mistakes are learning experiences.** Mistakes are signposts on the journey to innovation. If you're not making mistakes, you're probably not being innovative in your thinking. It takes bravery to try something new. Talk about times you've made mistakes and how you felt; these stories tell your team it's okay to try and there's no punishment for getting it wrong.

5. **Protect your team.** Sometimes things go wrong and ideas fall apart. As a leader, be prepared to take the blame if it comes. It's your role to nurture creativity and experimentation, which also means protecting them from the consequences of a failure. Not only will this inspire team loyalty, but your team will also work even harder at their ideas under your protection, leading to greater success.

6. **Find new ways to share ideas.** Not everyone will be comfortable with sharing their ideas in front of others. We're used to having our ideas criticised and having to defend them, and many good ideas are smothered or neglected. Don't rely on meetings to spark creativity. Have an ideas box, create a creativity space where people can add suggestions to a board as they think of them, and make yourself available to anyone who wants to share their ideas in private. Make the process as easy as possible, especially while your people build up their confidence in you and the new approach.

7. **Don't take over.** Resist the urge to take control of the process once the idea has been born. It's important the team has ownership of the idea right through to

completion. If they don't see the results of their work and experience the satisfaction that comes with it, they'll feel like nothing more than an idea incubator. That's a sure way to trample on their ability and willingness to create.

8. **Acknowledge and praise every idea.** Not all ideas will work or even make sense. It's important not to be critical of them or you risk shutting down the source. When you acknowledge every idea, you're reinforcing the creative process and motivating your people to keep thinking in this new way.

9. **Consider your environment.** Is your office filled with cubicles? Are people isolated from each other? Creativity is sparked when people are together. Think about changing the floor plan if you can do so without disrupting the flow of business. Even better, ask your team to explain how they'd like their workplace to look, and make those changes. If your layout options are limited, take your people off-site. Simply getting out of the office changes the mindset and frees up the thinking process. Many a great idea was born in a coffee shop or over lunch.

10. **Practice!** Remember that creativity needs to be continuously practiced so it embeds itself into normal life. It's not something that happens in a meeting or between three and five every Friday afternoon. Creativity is a free spirit. Allow your people time to explore their ideas. During meetings, if things seem to be falling back into the old ways, ask questions like, "Is

this the best way it could be done?" to jump-start the team's creativity.

Whether or not you're a creative person, you can be innovative. There are creative ideas and minds all around us just waiting for help being implemented. Just making the changes I've suggested will be innovative in your workplace. However, if you can create an environment which fosters creative thinking, recognises great ideas when they are born, and guides your team to adapt and implement them, you're certainly an innovative leader.

Leading an Adaptable and Innovative Business

In 2016, Adobe's research into creativity and business found that an investment in creativity results in improved competitiveness in the marketplace and greater productivity. This makes complete sense if you realise companies fail when they can't or won't adapt to change. To stay competitive in the marketplace, companies need to be able to recognise the need to change and be willing and able to quickly adapt. Adaptability applies to individuals as well as organisations. Those who are adaptive in nature lead their organisations to adapt to change.

Innovation is a strategy which can boost profits and increase employee engagement and motivation at work. An innovative business is likely to be a stronger one, future-proofed in a changing world.

Does that mean we need innovation for innovation's sake? No. An innovative business is one which focuses on continuous innovation, having new ideas, systems, or products on a regular basis. It's about being ahead of the need to change when possible. Innovation becomes an ongoing process of gradual change and growth aligned with current and future demands.

Let's assume that in your adaptable business you've created an environment and infrastructure which encourages creativity, and demonstrated your support of new ideas and experiments across the organisation. The ideas are flowing thick and fast. How can you use them to lead your business towards a sound future?

Make Innovation a Strategy

An innovative and adaptable business doesn't turn to innovation only when a problem arises. It encourages innovative thinking from the ground up. It should be part of your business model.

As an innovative business leader, you must develop a framework for your innovation processes to ensure they remain aligned with your business purpose and needs. Ask yourself these questions:

- What are we going to do?
- What external pressures/challenges/opportunities have we spotted?
- What internal pressures/challenges/opportunities have we spotted?
- How have our customers' buying habits changed?
- How have our customers' problems changed?
- What's the biggest problem our customer faces?
- Why are we doing it? (your main purpose/focus)

- **?** What do we want to achieve?

- **?** How will the innovation process work?

- **?** Who do we need to work with during the process (e.g. customers, designers)?

- **?** How will we measure the results?

Innovation is a strategy in the same way marketing is and it should be handled in the same way, with an understanding of market trends, social expectations, and customer needs. For innovation to be an effective strategy, you need to make it happen.

Pay Attention

Get out from behind the desk. Observe your customer. Identify any patterns that might provide insights into their needs. Innovation springs from observation and patterns. A prime example here is the headrest on planes. This idea came from a flight attendant who had watched passengers' heads drop every time they slept in flight and submitted the suggestion as a result.

Gain Insights

Speaking with your customers is a powerful way to unlock innovative ideas and adapt to changing marketing conditions. Ask them:

- **?** What frustrates you?

- **?** What problems do you have?

? What should we stop doing?

? What should we keep doing?

? What should we start doing?

Talking to customers is always a priority for an adaptable leader. Many leaders, particularly the old-school kind, tend to sit in their ivory towers. Too many leaders have not spoken to their customers in years. Without your customer, you don't have a business. Put the customer at the centre of everything you do and innovation will become an organic process in your organisation.

Manage Risk

Change involves a certain level of risk. Innovative managers are prepared to take risks, but they also prepare to handle the consequences if necessary. They understand the possible impact and assess it as manageable before following through.

Think Critically to Solve the Problem

Innovative leaders can think about possible outcomes and weigh up the associated risks before choosing an action. While it's important to look at a problem from different angles to create possible solutions, it's also important to look at those solutions, analyse them and foresee the possible consequences. It's this ability to assess the possible solutions which turns a creative solution into one that can be implemented.

Spot Opportunities

It isn't luck that provides opportunity; it's awareness. The ability to spot new opportunities is a key skill of the innovative leader. To give the business an advantage, develop the habit of looking for opportunities. Talk to industry experts, watch trends, listen to and observe clients, explore social media, look for gaps in your system or processes, ask about the biggest problems people face, and watch for unexpected changes, internal and external. Your subconscious mind is your ally in the process, picking up on cues you might otherwise have missed.

Use Diversity as a Tool

When you look at a problem or opportunity from different viewpoints, you build a more complete picture and can tap into a wider range of knowledge and experience to help generate new ideas. Build teams with people of different backgrounds, ages, and genders. Build teams of people who aren't necessarily employees. Why not invite customers to be part of your idea generation process? Creative solutions are born when you think differently.

Start Small

Innovation doesn't have a size so why not start small and let your people get the hang of it? Incremental innovation will give you results while you refine and introduce your innovation strategy. If you have a product, ask how it could be improved. If you offer a service, ask how it could be better. Start by building on the base you've already established. Get some success under your innovation belt and your team will want more.

Creativity and innovation are attitudes and key components of adaptability. No form of technology can replace the creative power of the human mind, especially when people are working together and willing to instigate change when necessary. Creativity and innovation can lead to a stronger brand, problem reduction, cost saving, and better profits. They're the power behind your capacity to adapt and not just survive, but to confidently forge a way ahead and take advantage of change instead of being threatened by it.

Build your strategy around your people and you'll reap the rewards with increased productivity, higher efficiency, higher employee engagement, and much more workplace satisfaction. Your ultimate success is in the hands of your people, so take good care of them.

CHAPTER TEN

Capitalise on Tomorrow – Critical Thinking

Do you remember a time before smartphones? What about your life before Facebook or the internet? Possibly not. By the year 2030, we'll have lost millions of jobs to automation and artificial intelligence. The new world will look very different to how it does today. Over the next decade the job market and professional landscape will change tremendously too. It'll look so different, we're unable to imagine it. The future workforce and leadership will rely on knowledge creation and innovation. Machines and artificial intelligence will provide freedom to experiment, explore, and find solutions to complex problems.

Critical Thinking Skills

Critical thinking skills such as problem solving, logical thinking, independent thinking, and adaptability will be essential to leadership success. The old-school management approach will no longer exist and leaders who can't adapt will be left behind. Critical thinking is about improving your thought processes by analysing, assessing, and rebuilding how you think. It involves thinking beyond autopilot in a self-aware and self-correcting mode. Critical thinking is thinking with intent and determination.

It's free of bias and based on conscious communication which comes from a place of humility, not ego. Critical thinking can be applied to any issue, situation, or subject matter.

Critical thinking matters because your thinking guides your actions and your choices, which impact your life, your work, and your leadership. Your thinking matters. Critical thinking is driven by exploration, self-discovery, and learning, and it counters bias.

Essentially, you are what you think. Your results, leadership, and life are all determined by the quality of your thinking. In this dynamic fast-paced world, the more critically you think, the more well-rounded and well-versed you will be. Over time, critical thinking shapes you into a logical, disciplined, and lateral thinker. It can reduce your biases and errors, minimise damages, and gives you a better grasp on the environment and market in which you operate. Most people don't consider how they think, or the reason for why they think the way they do.

Knowing is not enough. To use your critical thinking skills, you need to be able to analyse the known events, put the facts into a logical order, and have clarity around the reason for the specific event, situation or problem. To be proficient at critical thinking, you must have the skill to analyse data and issues so that you can make sense of the information. This will assist you in painting a picture of what's going on, and when you do this, you gain varied perspectives.

I was able to use my critical thinking skills when I was an executive in the travel industry, working in a new role as head of sales and marketing. I noticed when analysing the forward forecast for the business that it had been down at the same time the previous year. The company at this time did not analyse data to its full potential, and when I brought the information to the CEO, he dismissed it.

What's interesting here is that the company had spent many years as a key player in the industry; to believe sales could decline was not deemed feasible. The market was also in a growth phase so, on the surface, all looked good. However, I was sure something was going on that—without further investigation, knowledge and insight—would cause trouble.

It was at this time that I knew I had to improve my critical thinking skills so that I could walk into any situation (this one in particular) with the tools required to set my emotions aside (my frustration with my boss not seeing the market shifts). I needed to gather information to help others see past their unconscious biases. So how did I do this in a coherent manner? I broke it up into four steps.

Step One

My first task was to gather more information and analyse it. Analysing information is vital for critical thinking. No one can think critically all the time. Sometimes our frustrations or other emotions are too high and other times we struggle to focus on the fundamental issues.

In this situation, I gathered more data on the sales patterns. I could still see that the data was telling me a clear story that something was wrong, and sales were declining. I needed more information, so I went to the market and completed a critical study on buying habits of our clients (retail) and in turn the buying habits of their clients (the consumer).

What became evident was:

1. Our clients, the retail stores, were starting to shop around because the consumer was becoming more price conscious.

2. Consumer buying habits were changing because they could research and buy online.

3. The traditional industry was being disrupted which was beginning to cause chaos.

4. Many of the conventional operators were complacent and had their heads in the sand (many of these businesses didn't make it).

I could clearly understand what was happening but I needed to evaluate all the data, including our internal data, and think critically about how the information impacted the consumer, the retail stores, our business, and the bottom line.

Step Two

The second step was to present the information to the board. Here's what I learnt:

1. It's not possible to listen and think at the same time. Active listening is a critical skill.

2. To become a critical thinker, you must listen to others' ideas, criticisms, and argument without distraction and, most importantly, refrain from attempting to formulate a response while they are speaking. It was challenging for me at the time, as the board were not buying into the concerns I raised and again I was frustrated.

3. I learned to listen to what they had to say, which enabled me to see why they did not understand the issue.

4. Active listening allowed me to step into their shoes, to be empathetic towards them so I could better understand their position. This doesn't always mean their position is right.

I appreciated their struggle to comprehend the problem and I could see their perspective. I took that information and analysed how I could better articulate and present the data in an impactful way which would enable them to see the insights and the story the information told.

Step Three

From there, I needed to re-evaluate and become a critic of my thoughts and actions. I needed to reflect, to grow, and to change my tactic. Here's what I did next:

1. I reflected upon my thoughts, analysing why I believed the information was enough to demonstrate the problem, and how I could better present it so others were able to see the issue clearly and we could subsequently move on to problem solving.

2. I needed to assess the information objectively so I could clarify my thoughts and find a solid logic to what I believed, rather than relying on insights only I could see.

3. I asked myself, "Why do I understand what the data is showing me? Can I prove if this is true or false, and how have I reached this conclusion? Am I attached to my perspective? Why? Is there another perspective?"

When you're able to objectively self-reflect, you can see how you respond in situations. I collated the data differently and presented it in a way which was more objective, whilst understanding varied perspectives and arguments. This time the board understood our position, and we were able to move on to problem solving and implementing strategies to remain relevant. Had this not happened, we would have ended up as just another Blockbuster; a business model that didn't evolve with the rapidly changing markets and had neglected to remain relevant. The experience taught me that critical thinking wasn't much use if I couldn't communicate productively. Emotional intelligence also comes into play here since the foundation for communication is compassion. Compassion is the ability not only to view the perspectives and feel the emotions of others, but it's when those feelings and thoughts include a genuine desire to help. Another foundation is observation, and finally, collaboration.

Collaboration is an organic consequence of a person showing up with an open mind, compassion, and a strong focus on solving a problem, leaving their ego, their need to control, and any defensiveness at the door.

Step Four

The final step was to develop foresight, which is the ability to analyse the future impact of a decision or strategy.

1. Foresight is a crucial element to success. Don't mistake foresight for over-analysing. They are different. Overthinking can cause analysis paralysis, and no progress is ever made in this state of chaos. It's the biggest obstacle to decision making. Evaluate the potential impact of decisions before you make them to ensure you're heading in the right direction.

2. Every decision should be weighed up in both your personal life and your professional life. Foresight is powerful.

What's challenging for old-school leaders is the fact that critical thinking requires them to reflect on their own beliefs while considering other ideas, and then establish connections between the two. Old-school management is more dictatorial and directive; it's an approach with no place in future leadership. The main reason this style of management continues in many organisations is that they're still hiring people based on old practices. The transition has started, and it's happening faster than you can imagine. If you're a future leader, you'll be ready.

With these four steps, I was able to implement many vital strategies to ensure the business remained relevant. We grew the business by over 24 per cent in 18 months in a declining, heavily disrupted market, and we were one of the few businesses to survive. Many of our competitors went under within a year.

Five Critical Thinking Skills

Don't be left behind. Make sure you have the top five critical thinking skills required for the future of leadership.

1 – Analytical Skills

If you have analytical skills, you can examine information, understanding what it means and what it's telling you about what's going on. It's one of my superpowers. I see trends and insights most people don't. This skill has served me well and ensured I became a high performer.

In critical thinking, the steps you take to analyse allow you to differentiate and evaluate information. Learning occurs in three areas: cognitive, affective, and psychomotor. Cognitive analysis involves the process of distinguishing or separating. It allows you to get a better understanding by using your ability to break down complex items or ideas.

Some of the ways you can gather and analyse information are:

- Asking insightful questions

- Seeking information

- Analysing data

- Interpreting data and information

- Non-judgemental objective analysis

- Questioning the evidence

- Recognising different perspectives and similarities

- Challenging the status quo

2 – Creativity

Creativity is another skill that complements critical thinking. It enables you to see the picture the information paints, the patterns, and the possible solutions. All of this requires a creative eye. Creativity helps you to look at the situation differently and generate new solutions.

Creativity is:

- Vision

- Curiosity

- Cognitive flexibility

- Concept creation

- Imagination

- Abstract connections

- Prediction

- Integration

3 – Open-mindedness

To think critically, you need to keep an open mind. You must be unbiased; recognise your assumptions or judgements and purely analyse the information you receive. This allows you to be objective, evaluating ideas without bias. Open-mindedness is the virtue by which we learn. Having an open mind means considering relevant information, evidence, or arguments to revisit your current understanding. This includes embracing diverse perspectives.

An open mind:

- Is inclusive

- Is receptive

- Is humble

- Is impartial

- Is objective

- Examines

- Reflects

4 – Communication

Communication is an important tool in critical thinking. It's vital during the information gathering stage when you're doing your research, and during the analysis stage where you and your team are identifying what's really going on. When you finally share your conclusions with others, you'll need to be able to communicate your ideas and findings well.

Communication is crucial for:

- Asking important questions

- Compassion

- Assessment

- Collaboration

- Explanation

- Articulating opinions and ideas

- Presentation

- Verbal and written communication

5 – Solving Problems

Problem solving is an essential skill because you can't move forward until you overcome the problem in front of you. It entails analysing a problem, finding and implementing a solution, and measuring its effectiveness.

People thrive when they can think and solve problems. Challenges become opportunities. As a leader, you must be able to problem solve and think critically, and encourage your team to do so too.

Solving problems involves:

- Evaluation

- Logic

- Attention to detail

- Clarification

- Collaboration

- Evaluation

- Identifying patterns

- Innovation

- Decision making

Critical Thinking Process

There are four main stages of critical thinking:

Stage one is observation, which includes analysis, interpretation, and reflection upon the information collected.

Stage two involves the evaluation of the data or information collected and considering the insights and implications of it.

Stage three is problem solving, which identifies varied solutions and analyses the pros and cons for each. It involves considering the information from many perspectives.

The final stage is decision making, which involves deciding how to move forward, how you will implement, who is responsible for what and by what timeline, and finally, how and how often you measure progress.

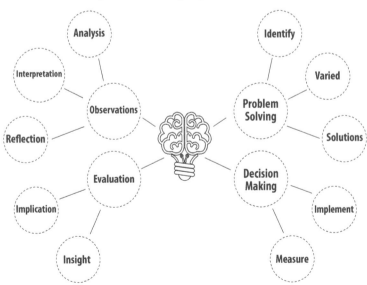

You need to be able to:

- ❏ Think about a subject or problem critically and objectively.

- ❏ Review the information and evaluate the various arguments.

- ❏ Reflect upon all the arguments.

- ❏ Evaluate the different points of view, determine how strong and valid they are and identify any areas of weakness.

- ❏ Evaluate the implications of each point of view and determine the validity of each.

- ❏ Assess the insights and collate structures, reasoning, and evidence for the argument you wish to make.

- ❏ Identify and provide reasoning and support for the proposed solutions. Consider with foresight any implications to the proposed solutions.

- ❏ Decide how you'll move forward.

> "The world as we've created it is a result of our thinking. It cannot be changed without changing our thinking first."
> – Albert Einstein

We perceive the world around us based on how we think, which governs our course of action.

Logic and Reasoning

Logical thinking involves a step-by-step process. It involves checking the different elements of the argument and looking at the connections and insights from them. This is called reasoning.

You might think logic and reason are the same, but they're not. Logic is a rule for developing a justifiable conclusion and is based on fact, for example, 5+5=10. This conclusion can be drawn based on rational rules and common theory. When statements don't follow any such premise, we call them illogical.

Logical thinking has four significant steps:

1. Asking the right questions.

2. Organising the information and data.

3. Evaluating the data.

4. Coming to a conclusion.

Let's look further into each of these steps.

Step One – Questions

One of the most important questions to ask is, "What are the assumptions?" If you make assumptions in critical thinking, further assumptions will be made throughout the process.

Here are some critical thinking questions:

- What is the information or data telling you? Explain with examples.

? What data and information is the most/least important? Why?

? What evidence can you present for/against?

? What is the significance of the information? Explain your reasoning.

? What are the benefits and disadvantages?

? What is the argument or big idea?

? How do you know the information is accurate?

? What other ideas could you add, and what would be their impact?

? What solutions could you suggest for the problem?

? What would be the most effective solution, and why? Explain with examples.

? What information do you need to make a decision?

? What are the patterns you're noticing? Explain with examples.

? What makes X important? Why?

Step Two – Organisation

The second step in the logical process is organising the information and data. You can start to arrange the information by making connections. Using diagrams or laying out the statements can be an effective way of organising information or data to see patterns. You can use charts to lump together the information that correlates. The following diagram is an example of how to visually show connections.

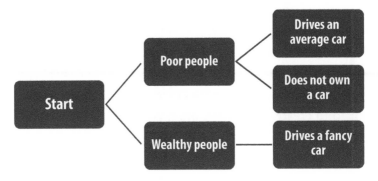

Step Three – Evaluation

The next step is evaluating the information. When you evaluate information, you're establishing if it's valid. You can't draw a conclusion until you're able to make a distinction between what is the truth and what is valid. Our ingrained beliefs and biases come into play here, and this is where people often struggle to separate what is valid from what is true. As human beings, we tend to use information to support our position or theory; this is called confirmation bias. It's not critical thinking. We see confirmation bias used a lot by old-school managers. They use the information to push their agenda. We must be wary of our own bias in order to leverage critical thinking and the new world of leadership.

Step Four – Conclusion

Finally, when the information or data is collated, organised, and evaluated, we can begin drawing conclusions backed up by evidence and logical reasoning. Insights naturally flow from evidence, and this is where you must challenge your assumptions, be aware of your bias, and check to ensure insights are consistent. If you don't, you'll move forward to the decision making and problem solving stage with incorrect information which will cause issues later. You don't want to lead your troops into a battlefield that you're not prepared for. Your critical thinking skills will make sure that doesn't happen.

Linear thinking is connected to logic, and non-linear thinking is linked to creativity. Our left brain governs our logical thinking, and our right brain governs our creativity.

Non-linear/Lateral Thinking

When we come across a problem, we usually gather the facts and sort them into a logical order. We follow them through and work toward a conclusion or solution. When we don't use this approach and we deviate from the logical order, it's called non-linear thinking. You might know this as lateral thinking. It involves thinking outside the box that our brains are usually stuck within.

Non-linear thinking doesn't come easily because it requires us to step out of our comfort zones. Doing this takes energy, so instead we take the path of least resistance and do what we've always done. However, only when we step out of our comfort zones do we allow our brains room to move and begin to see things from a different perspective. Non-linear thinking shakes things up and stimulates human creativity. Often this is where brilliant ideas are born.

A critical first step in solving any problem is to gather all the information. One of the biggest and most common mistakes I see is people or organisations jumping to conclusions before they have all the facts. A simple way to challenge people's thinking and ensure they have done all the necessary research is to ask, "How do you know that?"

Let's take a look at how we can use our understanding of logic to gather all of the essential facts.

We know change is happening. Right now, it's happening quickly. How well are your people adapting to each change? Honestly, it's a case of adapt and survive or stay as you are and fade away. A perfect example is how organisations, leaders, and employees had to adjust to the COVID19 restrictions across the world. We were all thrown into a sink-or-swim situation, and we needed to act fast to survive. I worked with top-level leaders and organisations over this time, and the ones that adapted quickly and without resistance fared the best.

An illustration of linear thinking in business is when you come up with products that are used daily, such as toothpaste. Non-linear thinking (lateral thinking) leads to innovative products that customers never knew they wanted, like the headrests on the planes, or mobile apps such as Uber and Canva.

Critical thinking skills are in high demand for the future. Essentially, companies want people whose leadership skills are well developed. Tomorrow's top leaders will need to think critically, innovate, solve problems, collaborate, and communicate more effectively than today's.

Exercise Time – Critical Thinking

Let's take a look at who you are as a leader and individual, and who we are as a society. The following exercises will help you to see what you do or what you value with a fresh perspective.

The first exercise is to stimulate your thinking beyond its usual scope, and the remaining activities are related to leadership and business, and are intended to stimulate your critical thinking skills.

Exercise One – Hosting Visitors from Outer Space

There are two hypothetical situations in which you are hosting visitors from outer space who are here to study earth. Use the situations and related questions to discover your assumptions, writing them down as you go.

Situation One

The alien visitors see cricket fans cheering on their team as they score a run. One of the visitors is a little curious and asks you the following questions. Think about how you would answer them.

- **?** Why are the humans cheering?

- **?** Why do people play sports?

- **?** Why hit a ball with a cricket bat?

- **?** How do you decide who wins?

- **?** Why are people focused on this game and not worried about other matters like global warming or poverty?

- **?** Why do humans get aggressive and emotional during these games?

- **?** What would happen if sports no longer existed?

Situation Two

You're in a restaurant and one of the visitors sees a story on the television about how different countries are handling COVID19. The visitor wants to know more, and asks you the following questions. Again, consider how you would answer each of them.

? Why are some countries in strict lockdown and others are not?

? Who makes the decisions and how?

? How do you know it's the right decision?

? Why do humans fight with each other about COVID19?

? In what other ways have humans tried to overcome this pandemic?

? How do you know which country has the correct approach?

? How does this pandemic affect humans?

? How could this have been handled differently?

Exercise Two – Analyse Your Competitors

Analysing your competitors not only expands your thinking but helps you create opportunities whereby you are one step ahead of the competition. You could analyse an organisation or perhaps a competitor in another industry. I used cross-industry innovation with augmented reality and applied it in the travel industry to gain a competitive advantage. In a crowded marketplace, the more information and insight you have at your fingertips, the greater the opportunity to gain an edge over your competitors.

Study your competitors and attempt to analyse their strategies. More importantly, analyse how and where they are successful or how they can get ahead of you. As you try to understand how and why they win and lose, you'll learn how to do the same for yourself and your organisation. You'll also identify opportunities for gaining an advantage over your competitors. A competitor can also be a colleague, or someone vying for the same role or promotion as you.

I remember decades ago receiving the best piece of advice from a mentor. He looked at me sternly and he said, "Success leaves clues. What do you want to achieve? Who's already achieved it? Are you studying and learning from the people who've already achieved what you want?"

This is a very powerful concept that successful people use every day. It's what Tony Robbins calls modelling psychology.

Exercise Three – Critical Thinking and Problem Solving

What keeps your boss or your board awake at night? Ask your boss or an executive/board member to lunch or have an informal meeting with them. If you're an executive who's looking to advance your career to the next level, use the opportunity to gain clarity around the vision, strategy, and direction of the business.

If you're a leader/executive of an organisation or department who's looking to deliver better results through innovative ideas or turning problems into opportunities, use the opportunity to ask questions about the key challenges they see for the organisation, and ask for their insights and observations. Task your team with solving a problem or an issue that comes up.

The aim here is for you to gain insight into the significant issues the business and its leaders struggle with every day. You will have greater clarity around the complex problems that are present, which you can then start to solve. Remember, challenges, issues, and obstacles are opportunities.

What Now?

Here's what you can do right now:

- ❏ Call a meeting with your team.
- ❏ Table the key problems you obtained from the meeting with your boss.
- ❏ Lead them through a structured problem solving session.

OR

If you're yet to identify the key problems:

- ❏ Call a meeting with your team.
- ❏ Ask, "What are the top three problems you're struggling with right now?" Ask them to evaluate problems in their departments. Look at each problem from multiple perspectives and work on developing solutions.
- ❏ Lead them through a structured problem solving session.

Your objective here is to turn problems into opportunities and guide your team through data gathering, analysis and countermeasure development.

The bottom line? You don't start running and expect your fitness to transform on day one. The same goes for leadership. Developing your leadership skills is a career-long activity. However, identifying and preparing leadership skills which are critical for the future is an excellent place to start.

CHAPTER ELEVEN

———

Looking at Things Differently – Creative Problem-solving

One of the most common misconceptions I hear is that leaders only manage the creative problem-solving efforts, as opposed to participating and leading the way. Nothing could be further from the truth; leaders play a crucial role in the creative problem-solving process.

The need for leadership development in this area has never been more urgent, as the workplace is changing fast, along with the skills in demand. Leaders must develop these skills, otherwise they'll be left behind. There is a need for everyone in business to step up and become a problem solver.

If you reflect upon any problem that you've experienced, I bet you've always found a way to deal with it. I'm sure with hindsight you may acknowledge that you've dealt with some problems better than others.

We all take a structured approach to problem solving but most people do it organically without realising. Your life experiences shape your responses to different scenarios, and your reactions have developed without any conscious awareness. As a result, we operate on autopilot in our approach to problem solving. We neglect to take the time to think and so we lack awareness as to why we are sometimes less successful than we could have been.

Not all problems are created equal. Some involve people, and some don't. Some are short-term, and some take a long time to solve. Here's a useful way of sorting work problems, based on the work of a management expert called Igor Ansoff.

1. Strategic problems are long-term wide-ranging issues that have significant consequences for the organisation as a whole.

2. Operational matters are usually medium- to short-term and involve the management of resources to achieve objectives.

3. Administrative problems are typically short-term or have a right or wrong answer according to the policies and procedures of the organisation.

The time you spend on strategic, operational and administrative problems depends on your leadership level. The allocation of time is critical for leaders to improve department/organisational performance and intensify their impact. But it's a common area where leaders fail because they are working harder rather than smarter.

Assess your current level of leadership and where you need to improve your allocation of time.

Level	Focus	Who	% Tactical	% Strategic
Organisation leader	Vision and strategy	CEO/MD	10	90
Department leader	Align and amplify performance	Senior executives	25	75
Leader of leaders	Model and coach	Leaders of managers, professional staff	50	50
Team leader	Develop and elevate	Leaders of individual contributors	75	25
Individual contributor	Motivate and train	Individual contributors, emerging leaders	95	5

Reflection Time

? What is your current level of leadership?

? What skills do you need to hone for your current level?

? What do you need to develop to successfully lead at the next level?

? Are you balancing the right proportions of management and leadership skills?

? If not, what can you do to shift your workload?

Divergent and Convergent Thinking

Divergent and convergent thinking strategies are two ways in which you can generate ideas and solve problems. Divergent thinking is associated with creative skills, and convergent thinking is related to analytical skills. Most leaders are well versed in analytics but don't excel at developing ideas or creating a culture in which it's safe and empowering to come up with ideas.

Divergent and convergent thinking are different ways of formulating ideas and result in different approaches to following those ideas.

Exercise – Stretch!

A Harvard University professor, Anne Manning, explains divergent and convergent thinking through an exercise which you can try now if you're in an appropriate space to do so. First, stand up and reach your hands up towards the sky. Keep reaching for a few seconds. Then, bend down to touch your toes. Keep trying to touch them.

How did it feel to reach up? Expansive, empowering, and energising, right? How did bending over to touch your toes feel? Restrictive, heavy, more constrained than when you were reaching up, right? I'm sure you can work out which action belongs with which type of thinking.

Here's more explanation which will help.

Divergent thinking is coming up with many ideas or solutions. It's about exploring possibilities to solve a problem. You start with a problem/point and you generate a variety of unique solutions. When you want to come up with new ideas, you have to go where you've not gone before; you have to go to an open space where there are no limits.

DIVERGENT THINKING

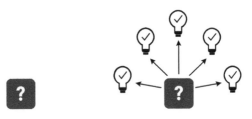

Begins with a problem/point.   **Generates varied solutions.**

Convergent thinking involves finding the single best solution to a problem. It's about taking multiple ideas and solutions, assessing them, pondering and reflecting on them, refining them, and formulating a decision on how to move forward. It works by starting with pieces of information and converging around a solution.

CONVERGENT THINKING

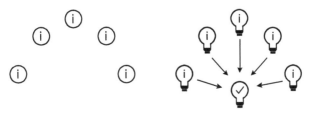

Begins with information.   **Converges on a solution.**

Coming up with ideas and making a decision are very different things, however, most of us try to do both at the same time. Imagine this common circumstance: you've requested ideas in a meeting, someone has made a suggestion, and Jonny has responded, "Oh, we tried that before" or, "It doesn't work", maybe even, "That's not possible" or, "We don't have the budget for that."

Jonny's effectively just killed any chance of a culture in which it's safe and empowering to come up with ideas. This immediate disparagement kills any chance of a culture of empowerment or innovation, and destroys the possibility of a thriving future.

We can't reach for the moon and touch the floor simultaneously, so why do we try to combine divergent and convergent thinking strategies? It keeps people stuck and limits their thinking.

Convergent Thinking Begins with Information

If you need to develop your convergent or analytical skills, or help someone else improve theirs, I'd recommend improving your ability to gauge timelines. When you're at the planning stages of a project, calculate how much time it will take you to complete it. Assess all the information and decide on a timeline, then, strive to complete the project on schedule.

It's also essential to learn more about finance. Ask questions about annual reports and budgets. Meet with a finance expert, take a course, or read a book about improving your commercial acumen and financial concepts. Again, convergent thinking starts with information and converges on a solution.

Convergent Thinking in Business

Learning how to read, understand, and gain insights from financial reports helped me immensely in having a broad range of skills that allowed me to take a multi-dimensional view of problems or situations.

I worked with an executive who continually told himself that he wasn't good with numbers, closing himself off from gaining these skills. He chose not to understand numbers, missing out on the insights and the story they tell you. He was overlooked for an MD position as a result. You need both convergent and divergent thinking as a leader.

Exercise – Identify Patterns

For the next week, I'd like you to keep a record of the problems you solve and how you solved them. Identify any patterns in your problem solving methodology. In the notes section, keep a record of the results/outcome of each decision or solution. It will be interesting to see if you're using divergent and convergent separately or at the same time.

Problem Solved	Divergent Thinking	Convergent Thinking	Notes

Exercise – What If?

If you need to develop your imaginative or divergent thinking, engage in 'what if' thought. Problem solving starts by asking 'what if' questions. Questions like, "What if the market changes, and my revenue stream no longer exists?" (a question the CEO of Blockbuster might have found useful in his time).

Two entrepreneurs, Marc Randolph and Reed Hastings, who were CEOs of Netflix, proposed a partnership twenty years ago to John Antioco, the CEO of Blockbuster. They suggested Blockbuster enter the online space by buying their company. Randolph describes Antioco as struggling not to laugh when they suggested a price of $50 million for their struggling company. Unfortunately for Blockbuster, Antioco underestimated the power of the online world and overlooked the younger company's place in it. He turned down the deal and now Netflix is worth billions while Blockbuster has folded. Blockbuster's CEO let his history of success allow him to become complacent. Complacency is the enemy of adaptability.

Assess your adaptability and problem solving skills by questioning whether you:

- ❏ See problems as opportunities for innovation.

- ❏ Continuously seek new ways of doing things.

- ❏ Actively ask 'what if' questions to yourself and your team.

- ❏ Like to explore new ideas.

- ❏ Proactively seek out what might challenge you and your team next.

- ☐ Shift gears with ease.

- ☐ Think about new and different ways you can accomplish your objectives.

Ask yourself the important 'what if' questions. Consider the possibilities for you in both your professional and personal life. Go to music, art, acting, or improvisation classes. Music is known to stimulate both the right and left brain function, regardless of personality stereotypes.

Exercise – Possibilities

Whenever you can, take the time to imagine the possibilities surrounding an object. How many different uses can you find for a necktie, or a hair tie? If you feel like you're not creative enough, surround yourself with people who are more creative than you. Observe and listen to them. What are their habits? Observe them in both their professional and personal lives and ask them about their capacities. Experiment with applying these new observations and insights into your own life.

Think It Through

Using the divergent followed by the convergent thinking process can prevent you from jumping to conclusions. Of course, there will be times when the problem is a simple administrative or operational one which may require a yes or no answer, and you don't want to spend lots of unnecessary time. However, for all other problems, you will likely want to spend more time diverging before you converge on your solution and plan of action.

When tackling problems, it's useful not to jump to a conclusion regarding the best solution, and if you're leading people, please don't rush into solving the problem for them. Help them find the solutions themselves. When leaders solve problems for their teams, they're not helping themselves or their teams because they're neglecting to care about improving people's thinking. The first stage of problem solving (unless the problem is very straightforward) is to generate several possible approaches and then think about which one is best.

Brainstorming

Brainstorming is the title often given to the process of trying to develop a range of ideas before selecting an option. When brainstorming, clarify the problem that you want to address. For example, you want to get to Sydney for a morning meeting next week. Brainstorm options. Do you travel by car, train, bus, or plane? It'll depend on where you live. Do you go down the night before, or stay on the night of the meeting before you return? Or perhaps you travel there and back on the same day?

Brainstorming is about being creative and not automatically dismissing a particular option because it seems difficult or impracticable. I talked earlier about the time in the meeting where Jonny came up with reasons why an idea was not possible—don't allow this to occur. It's the human default, and it breeds complacency.

For example, some people won't want to fly to Sydney for a day meeting, whilst for others it's a more viable alternative to staying overnight. After the brainstorming has taken place, you need to start selecting options. Think about limiting factors that will help to prioritise the best options; these might include family commitments, budget, and the timing of the various transport possibilities.

To make an informed decision, shortlist two or three possible options, get more details on the critical factors and compare each. All you can do is make the best decision at that time given the information available and be prepared to change your plans if the situation changes. We don't always make the right decision; that's okay. It's better to decide than to procrastinate. I see many people (including leaders) procrastinate on decision making, which stalls progress and frustrates those around them.

We are only as good as the team around us. How effective is your team or organisation at solving problems? Do you see evidence that problem solving is occurring, and it is following a logical process? How often do you jump to conclusions?

Creative Thinking

Let's talk about creative thinking. There are several ways you can help yourself and your team to organise information and ideas when you're trying make a decision and solve a problem. You can use tools from experts, such as Edward de Bono's "Lateral Thinking" and Tony Buzan's "Mind Mapping". Most tools involve presenting information in a way that displays identifiable links.

Using such approaches may increase your creativity. They encourage you to list the variety of information and go on to help you organise the data into connected groups.

Example – Travel Company

Let me tell you about one of the problems I experienced as a CEO. We were a wholesale travel company that produced brochures for travel agents, our trade partners, to distribute.

We had many competitors, so we were not in direct control of which brochures the travel agents handed out to the consumer. Therefore, we were very reliant on the travel agent choosing our brochure over our competitors'. The travel agent would hand out a brochure based on a variety of factors. Perhaps the choice came as a result of their relationship with the company, it could have been the commercial terms, overrides targets, or it could have been about choosing the best product for their client.

In a more commoditised market with the disruption of online travel sites, continuing to print these brochures was our largest cost. So, we needed to try and influence the travel agent's decision to give our brochure out over our competitors'.

There were many ideas thrown around in our brainstorming session. We dismissed no idea; there was none too big or too small, and we considered them all. We involved not just the executive team; we asked all our staff to submit ideas, and we listened to all of them. It was our divergent thinking process that aided us in coming up with varied ideas and solutions and exploring possibilities.

We then moved on to the convergent thinking process, taking those ideas and solutions, thinking about them, pondering and reflecting upon them, expanding and improving them, and coming up with a decision on how to move forward.

We decided to use cross-industry technology—augmented reality. We became the first travel company in the region to offer customers an innovative new way to plan holidays using augmented reality technology. Featured across our entire brochure front cover, the locally developed technology allows travellers to view an inspirational and aspirational 90-second video on each of our destinations via their smartphone.

The ease of using the app enhanced the traveller's research process and encouraged the travel agent to hand out our brochure because we had a point of difference. Augmented reality immersed the consumer in the real-world environment by connecting them to destinations and experiences. Travellers could momentarily immerse themselves in what they'd experience when they took their dream holiday. They could travel the world without leaving home.

It's one example of how we used our problem solving skills to innovate and grow our business. It worked. Our brochures were handed out to more people and we sold more holidays as a result. We were bucking the trend for growth when many of our competitors were declining.

Group Problem Solving

Where problem solving involves a group of people, the whole process can get much more complicated and time-consuming. If the problem is, like ours was, a strategic one which is broad ranging and affecting the entire or majority of an organisation, then a political process will almost inevitably need to take place in order to resolve the problem and make the decision.

The entire process will often take considerable time and the final decision may not suit everybody. The reality is that when there are considerations and contact with different individuals, you must consider a political dimension. Many managers and leaders get frustrated if they fail to appreciate this fact. When trying to solve a problem as a group, the same process of divergent and convergent thinking can be used.

You can generate a broader range of ideas from group brainstorming sessions, however, you might run into some problems when the group tries to agree on options. Different people may have different perspectives, and this may lead to conflict and disagreements. It's often essential to gain people's commitment to an approach before implementing it. Therefore, a consultation process may well be required. No matter what, a decision needs to be made either by the person with the necessary authority, by voting, or by group consensus.

As the leader, you'll want to ensure that once you've gained clarity around the problem and a suitable decision has been made about how to tackle it, then the action is taken. Proper time management and delegation practice are vital to ensure that you implement the solutions and the problem is solved. If not, it will return to haunt you and could even be worse than it was in the first place.

In many cases, you will need or want to record the agreed objectives and actions so that they can be reviewed in future, perhaps at a team meeting or an appraisal discussion. The record might be team meeting minutes, an email, a brief with a copy for stakeholders, or even a formal report. It's wise to follow the SMART objective rule to ensure all actions get implemented.

Seven Critical Steps in Problem Solving

To be effective in problem solving, creative thinking alongside a logical and disciplined approach is essential. There are seven critical steps in practical problem solving. You'll have noticed these in the example I shared.

1. Identify the problem.

2. Explore the problem. Specify the cause, the reasons, and the effects.

3. Identify and set objectives.

4. Identify possible solutions.

5. Evaluate and look for alternatives, select the most promising solutions.

6. Implement the solution.

7. Measure the impact.

As you will know, identifying the problem is more complicated than it sounds. We often treat symptoms, not causes, because time always seems to be in short supply. It leads us to skip this first essential step. When you feel you have identified the real problem, set it down on paper in no more than two sentences.

Specify the causes, reasons, and effects. There may be more than one cause; write the others down too. Specify the impact. If it's likely that other people will be involved, ensure you set the correct expectation up front. Defensive and negative attitudes hinder progress or improvement.

As mentioned earlier, to explore all possibilities and ideas, you may use brainstorming. Evaluate and select the most promising solutions.

Select the most promising options and ideas and measure their relative value. We're now in the convergent thinking process, taking those ideas and solutions, considering, pondering and reflecting on them, refining and improving them, and deciding how to move forward.

Plan the Action and Action the Plan

This plan should include:

- ☐ A timeline, responsibilities, and a schedule with regular follow-up on progress.

- ☐ Who is doing what and by when, alongside how you'll measure if the activity is successful.

- ☐ Your definition of success.

Cause and Effect

Cause and effect is a method which helps to detect all the likely sources of a problem. When done right, you fix the problem the first time around and it won't keep coming back to bite you on the bottom.

You would use this technique when seeking the root cause of a problem. When you first look at the cause, it's tempting to find quick fixes or temporary solutions, which usually don't solve the problem. A cause and effect analysis allows you to understand the problem and consider all the options thoroughly. It also points to possible areas for data collection.

The diagrams created using this type of analysis are also known as fishbone diagrams because they look like a fish skeleton. They are the brainchild of Professor Ishikawa.

FISHBONE DIAGRAM

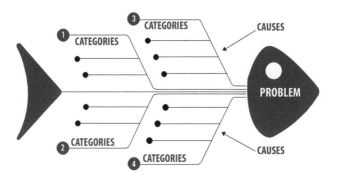

This diagram is used in understanding all the potential causes of a problem. Arranging the information according to its level of importance or detail allows you to picture the relationships and hierarchy of events. When using this technique to solve your problem, break your issue down into categories. Some of the most common in business are material, systems, equipment, employees, environment, customers, and so on. You can use these categories as a guide, but the types you select should be tailored to your needs.

If you look at mind mapping, you can also see how to use tree diagrams. A tree diagram may be easier to use when solving increasingly complex problems. With the tree structure, ensure all items on the same level are aligned vertically, so visually it is easier to read.

You'll see there are several parallel lines that extend outward from each category. Use these to document possible causes and reasons for the problem in relation to each.

Example Problem – Staff Turnover

Staff turnover is a common issue for businesses, so we'll use it in this example.

The possible factors are:

- Leadership

- Workplace culture and environment

- Opportunities for training and development

- Opportunities for promotion

- Succession planning

- Remuneration

- Workplace flexibility

To successfully build the cause and effect diagram, ensure from the beginning that you all agree on the problem and the impact. Be concise. Think about the causes for each of the categories and add them to the sub-elements. Pursue all the issues back to their root cause. Split up overcrowded problems into separate categories. Contemplate which of the root causes warrant further investigation.

Steps to Apply to All Problem Solving Experiences

We've talked about a few of the techniques that can be used in problem solving, but there are many others, such as:

- Matrix analysis

- Paired comparison

- Team purpose analysis

- SWOT analysis

- The five Ws

- The six thinking hats

I teach many of these techniques in my creative problem-solving training programs. However, you've probably realised by now that all techniques share numerous individual steps that you can integrate and apply to all problem solving situations.

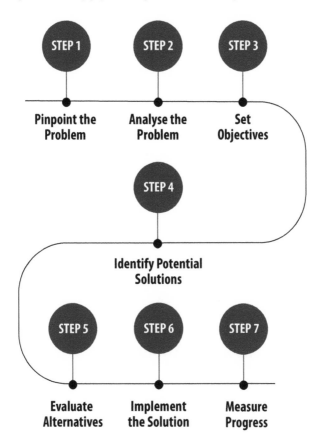

Step One – Pinpoint the Problem

Identifying the problem is the first step. While this may sound pretty simple; it isn't because a lot of the time people are not even aware that there is a problem. Problems are opportunities in business, and problem solving needs to be built into the DNA of your leadership. Ask your team to regularly come up with their top three problems and turn them into opportunities. As mentioned earlier, ensure you help them push past the stock answer. Techniques for identifying issues include:

- Analysing complaint patterns

- Analysing mistake patterns

- Comparing your current performance with past performance

- Comparing your current performance against your targets or objectives

- Comparing performance against benchmarks

- Asking employees

- Market research

- Brainstorming

Step Two – Analyse the Problem

The next step, once you've pinpointed the problem, is to start to understand and establish the root cause. Remember, in the example

I shared the root cause was that all the brochures produced (by us and our competitors) lacked any real stand-out factors, they were just like everyone else's.

One of the biggest obstacles of problem solving is failing to thoroughly analyse and identify the root cause of a problem and instead getting caught up in the symptoms or effects, unable to progress. It's essential to focus on analysing and discovering the real cause of the problem, not just the issues or symptoms. To keep it simple, use the 5W1H (who, what, where, when, why, how) method of asking questions. To help you explore the problem in depth, start by discovering the answers for the following 5W1H questions.

Who?

? Who is involved?

? Who caused/is causing the problem?

? Who identified the problem?

? Who is it impacting?

? Who has already addressed this problem?

? Who are the experts around the problem?

? Who can help solve the problem?

? Who needs to know?

? Who should the problem be communicated to?

What?

- **?** What happened?
- **?** What are the causes?
- **?** What are the key indicators?
- **?** What is the specific cost or impact for us?
- **?** What is the cost or impact for others?
- **?** What have we tried?
- **?** What have we not tried?
- **?** What are we pretending not to know?
- **?** What have we considered but not tried yet?
- **?** What part needs more information?
- **?** What is it that's noticeable?
- **?** What kind of pattern is noticeable?
- **?** What are we trying to achieve?
- **?** What have/are others doing?
- **?** What can we do?
- **?** What should we communicate?

When?

? When did it happen?

? When did it first happen?

? When did it last happen?

? When did it come to our attention?

? When does it need addressing?

? When should the problem be communicated?

Where?

? Where is the problem happening?

? Where did it take place?

? Where did it have an effect?

? Where else is it happening?

? Where should we communicate?

Why?

? Why did it happen?

? Why do you think it happened (if you don't know for sure)?

? Why is it a problem?

? Why were no steps taken to prevent the problem from happening?

- **?** Why was no one able to rectify the issue earlier?

- **?** Why is a response needed now?

- **?** Why are our assumptions valid?

How?

- **?** How did it happen?

- **?** How was it noticed?

- **?** How often is it happening?

- **?** How are others handing this issue or similar issues?

- **?** How do you know it's an issue?

- **?** How should you communicate?

- **?** How do you move forward?

Step Three – Set Objectives

Once you've identified and analysed the problem, it's wise to set an objective that focuses on what should be the successful outcome. Again, we wanted our brochures to have a point of difference, a talking point so that travel agents would hand them out before any of our competitors'. When you create and document a goal objective, it provides clarity on the direction and focuses on a definitive outcome.

You're building stepping-stones towards the objective; clear goals which make the journey measurable. Use the SMART goals method (specific, measurable, achievable, realistic, and timely) as it increases the likelihood of a successful outcome.

Step Four – Identify Potential Solutions

At this point, you shift focus to exhausting the potential solutions and shortlisting the most viable. The expression 'two heads are better than one' is apt here. When a group of people search for a solution, they're more likely to come up with a greater variety of solutions when compared with working alone. Thus, group brainstorming aids in the problem solving process.

To help you discover and shortlist potential solutions:

❐ Ask probing questions.

❐ Analyse cross-industry solutions.

❐ Analyse cross-country solutions.

❐ Discuss and brainstorm ideas with others.

❐ Discuss with mentors.

Step Five – Evaluate and Look for Alternatives, Elect the Most Promising Solution

Now that you've shortlisted a range of solutions, you need to choose the most viable option to fix the problem, incorporating the insights you have learned about the issue to make an informed decision. Remember to assess if there are other alternatives, too. This is the convergent thinking process, taking those ideas and solutions, evaluating them, reflecting on them, refining them, and finally formulating the way forward.

Step Six – Implement the Solution

Nothing changes if nothing changes, which is why the implementation stage is the most critical of the process. Because, without implementation or action, nothing changes. Before applying the chosen solution, it's wise to document an action plan (it doesn't need to be a twenty-page document; a one-page action plan will suffice). A record ensures all key stakeholders are clear on the process. It also ensures everyone's responsibilities and provides clarity to the broader communication process, supporting greater accountability at every level. Here are some planning considerations:

- **?** What's the problem declaration? Clearly articulate the problem.

- **?** How will it impact you and your team?

- **?** What's the thought process behind the solution?

- **?** How will it impact individuals?

- **?** What are the benefits expected for the organisation?

- **?** What are the benefits expected for everyone?

- **?** How will the plan be implemented, when, and by whom?

- **?** What are the expected outcomes?

? How will it be measured, and by whom?

? How will the progress be reported to key stakeholders, and what's the timeline?

Step Seven – Measure Progress

All strategies implemented must be regularly measured and evaluated. It's the step that many people neglect, yet it's one of the most important. You can't claim or recognise success unless you assess and review the success and progress of the solution against your anticipated outcomes. What gets measured improves, and you don't know if it's effective unless you measure progress towards the objective.

? Did the solution work, based on your objective?

? If no, why not?

? If yes, why?

? What worked well and what didn't?

? What did you learn?

? What do you need to adjust to make the solution more effective?

? When will you measure it again?

? What are your expectations when you next measure it?

Exercise – Leadership Problem Solving

Following are exercises intended to encourage you to problem solve as a leader and consider what problems you could solve in your organisation. Start with a known problem and use the steps below.

Seven Steps	Detail
Pinpoint the problem	
Analyse the problem	
Set objectives	
Identify potential solutions	
Evaluate and look for alternatives, and elect the most promising solution	
Implement the solution	
Measure progress	

When leading people in organisations where problems persist and remain unresolved, the following will most likely arise:

- Staff become demotivated

- Customers purchase elsewhere

- Resources are wasted

- Revenue declines

- Profit is reduced

- Compromised growth/survival risk

Solving a problem usually removes an obstacle to high performance, which leads to:

- Increased productivity

- Revenue growth

- Increased profits

- Increased satisfaction

- Reduced stress

- Enhanced quality of work

- Enhanced efficiency

- Maintained relevance

- Innovation

We all operate in a rapidly changing market which presents challenges to most industries. Therefore, we all must improve our problem solving behaviour and skills. Artificial intelligence already helps humans to solve some problems, but it can't solve everything. Therefore, your skills must evolve to meet the needs of the future of leadership, and the future of leadership will demand more creative problem-solving skills.

The Nine Skill Accelerators Summary

In this book I've covered nine skill accelerators over three primary elements: leading self, leading others and leading business. I've explained why each skill is critical to leadership now and in the future, and provided examples and tools that you can use to assess your competence against each. It's time for you to honestly assess your skill levels for each of the nine accelerators if you want to remain relevant and increase your leadership impact now and into the future.

The future is unclear (COVID19 has seen to that!). We can't predict the world of work with any certainty. What we can say, however, is that these critical skill accelerators will be even more necessary than they are today. One thing which is predictable is human nature.

Your team and organisation will need strong, creative, emotionally intelligent leaders who understand human need and emotion. They'll need leaders who are willing to invest time and effort into improving team and individual skills. They'll need leaders who can communicate their vision and engage others in working towards it, no matter where they are.

No longer should you pause before making an investment in yourself whether it costs you time or money. It's something we should all be doing as a matter of course, but for leaders it's non-negotiable. Only by building your self-awareness do you learn to question the status quo of how you think and react, and how the world around you operates.

Without developing these nine skill accelerators, my career would not have flourished. I would not have been ready to respond creatively to challenges nor would I have discovered talents I didn't know I had. This will happen for you, too. Your abilities will be strengthened, you will trust in yourself, and you will have a positive impact on even the most challenging situations.

Where to now? If you haven't already done so, go back through the book and do the self-assessments. Don't just scan over them; take your time and consider your responses—you deserve your own honesty.

Next, find the best way for you to improve on your skillset. Think about practical ways of developing those skills, perhaps through mentoring, on-the-job training, project leadership, or coaching. Ask for feedback from the people you work with and from those leaders you admire. Don't hesitate. The people who matter will respect you for consciously working on your personal and professional development.

Alexander the Great is reported to have said:

"I am not afraid of an army of lions led by a sheep; I am afraid of an army of sheep led by a lion."

An army led by a sheep won't go anywhere, because sheep are timid creatures who won't take risks to save themselves or their flock. They don't lead; they just do what everyone else does. On the other hand, an army of sheep will follow a leader who is willing to lead, willing to act, and willing to take them in the right direction. It's the leader who makes or breaks the team. Are you a sheep or a lion?

If you want to be a lion—a leader with impact well into the future—put everything you've learnt here into practice. Don't wait, because time won't wait for you. Change is already happening. Your leadership skills are needed!

If you've enjoyed what you've read here, stay in touch by visiting my website www.carolinekennedy.com.au where I'll keep sharing important tips and strategies for leaders who want to make a real difference in the world.

ABOUT THE AUTHOR

Caroline Kennedy is an accomplished CEO, author, speaker, executive coach, board advisor and leadership futurist with over 25 years' leadership, mentoring and coaching experience.

As an executive coach, Caroline draws on her extensive background in business and leadership. She brings a multi-dimensional approach which combines coaching, mentoring and consulting methodology to break comfort zones and facilitate long-term growth and development.

Caroline's methods of coaching are neuroscience-based to achieve rapid high-performance. Her approach is honest and constructive, which yields fast results for growth or change. As one of the top international coaches, Caroline has clients across the globe.

Caroline specialises in working with ambitious individuals and organisations who are already very successful and hungry to realise more of their potential. She coaches executive management, managing directors, CEOs, engineering directors, directors in the education space, medical executives, and tech and IT owners, to name a few examples, and has worked with companies such as Deloitte, PWC, CBA, Cox & Kings Ltd, Flight Centre, Rydges, Fortune 500 listed companies and more.

Caroline has led multinational companies with annual revenues up to $250 million. She has delivered outcomes such as taking a company from $38 million to $50 million in 18 months during the global financial crisis. Caroline consistently delivers superior financial returns in challenging and highly competitive environments and declining markets. As an experienced CEO, Caroline has had the privilege of leading over 500 staff via ten direct reports. Her forte is creating high-performing teams and she has a natural talent for seeing patterns and insights that others don't, which propels both leadership and business performance.

The Telstra Business Women's Awards honoured Caroline twice for her achievements in business and leadership, and she received an International Stevie Award in 2019.

She's an avid trend-watcher who's contributed to publications such as The CEO Magazine, HuffingtonPost, Chamber of Commerce & Industry Queensland, and Empowering Ambitious Women.

Caroline has helped hundreds of managers, CEOs, MDs and directors to break through and take their impact and performance to another level, regardless of their previous level of success.

To find out more about Caroline, visit www.carolinekennedy.com.au or email her directly on caroline@carolinekennedy.com.au

WORK WITH CAROLINE

It is Caroline's hope that at least one or two of the ideas in this book resonate strongly with you.

Developing your leadership skills is one of the most valuable investments you'll ever make in yourself.

When you're ready to intensify your impact and performance, reach out! It would be Caroline's privilege to guide you on this journey because it has the potential to change your career and life forever. This might sound like a bold statement, but many people have transformed their leadership, their career, and their success through coaching.

KEYNOTE SPEAKING
Caroline is an engaging and passionate speaker who can connect with any audience. She places importance on being able to speak from the heart with complete authenticity and authority.

Caroline has helped hundreds of people leverage their leadership with her speeches on emotional intelligence, high performance, leadership, innovation, navigating uncertainty, business growth, confidence, resilience and courage.

Her inspiring and energising keynotes blend practical, evidence-based strategies with unforgettable stories and authenticity, making her a conference favourite.

Find out more at www.carolinekennedy.com.au/speaker

ORGANISATIONAL EDUCATION AND TRAINING
Want to ensure leaders in your organisation, along with their teams, are as effective as possible and performing to a high standard?

Caroline teaches your leaders to apply evidence-based leadership theory practically. Her leadership development training is evidence-based methodology from human behavioural science, neuroscience and management theory.

ONLINE COURSES
Using the CK Method, Caroline has created the practical online master-influencing program. Success leaves clues, so accelerate your success by learning from those who've walked the path before you.

Caroline only teaches what she's practised successfully in her career and life, and she's been teaching the same fail-safe processes, techniques and skills for years to those she's coached and mentored. Spoiler alert: influencing comes up in almost every coaching session Caroline facilitates.

Find out more at www.carolinekennedy.com.au

PRIVATE CONSULTING, EXECUTIVE COACHING AND MENTORING
Caroline mentors CEOs, executives and highly ambitious people from Australia and all around the world. She's often asked by leaders

to be a sounding board, given her background in the C-suite. These already successful leaders seek Caroline for advice, an alternative perspective, or someone to stretch their thinking.

Coaching is an effective and powerful opportunity to enhance your potential, your leadership, your impact and your performance. Caroline's methods of coaching are neuroscience and human behaviour based to achieve rapid high-performance. Her approach is honest and constructive, which yields fast results for growth, change and impact.

Caroline is in her element, working one-on-one with executives. She knows all too well that there's no 'one size fits all'. She gives you her sole attention, and guidance tailored to your specific needs to achieve rapid personal and professional development.

Find out more at www.carolinekennedy.com.au/executive-coach

References:

Ansoff, H. I., Kipley, D., Lewis, A. O., Helm-Stevens, R., & Ansoff, R. (2018). Implanting strategic management. Springer.

Arora, J. (2017). Corporate governance: a farce at Volkswagen?. The CASE Journal.

Baldoni, J. (2010). 12 Steps to Power Presence: How to Assert Your Authority to Lead. AMACOM Div American Mgmt Assn.

Baldoni, J. (2013). The Leader's Guide to Speaking with Presence: How to Project Confidence, Conviction, and Authority. Amacom.

Bar-On, R. (2006). The Bar-On model of emotional-social intelligence (ESI). Psicothema, 18, 13-25.

Baumgartner, J. (2010). The Way of the Innovation Master. JPB Bwiti.

Boyatzis, R. E., & Goleman, D. (1999). Emotional competence inventory. Boston: HayGroup.

Bradberry, T., & Greaves, J. (2009). Emotional Intelligence 2.0. TalentSmart

Bradberry, T., & Tasler, N. (2014). Increasing your salary with emotional intelligence. Talent Smart.

Bradberry, T., Su, L. D., & Arora, S. (2007). Emotional intelligence and transformational leadership. http://www. talentsmart. com/media/uploads/ pdfs/EQ_Transformational_Leadership. pdf.

Buzan, T. (2006). Mind mapping. Pearson Education.

Cherniss, C., & Goleman, D. (2001). The emotionally intelligent workplace. How to select for, measure and improve emotional intelligence in individuals, groups and organizations san Francisco: Jossey-Bass.

Dagley, G. (2013). Executive presence: Influence beyond authority. Australian Human Resources Institute Review, 3, 1-17.

Davis, D. (2015). Where do I start.

De Bono, E. (1971). The Use of Lateral Thinking. Penguin Books.

De Bono, E. (1987). Six Thinking Hats. Penguin Books.

Einstein, A. (1987). The Collected Papers of Albert Einstein, Volume 13: The Berlin Years: Writings & Correspondence, January 1922-March 1923 (English Translation Supplement) (Vol. 13). Princeton University Press.

Eurich, T. (2018). What self-awareness really is (and how to cultivate it). Harvard Business Review.

Fox, R. L. (2004). Alexander the great. Penguin UK.

George, B., Ibarra, H., Goffee, R., & Jones, G. (2017). Authentic leadership (HBR Emotional Intelligence Series). Harvard Business Press.

Goffee, R., & Jones, G. (2001). Why Should Anyone Be Led by You?. IEEE Engineering Management Review, 29(1), 94-100.

Goldberg, E. (2002). Executive Brain: Frontal lobes and the civilized mind. Oxford University Press, USA.

Goleman, D. (2006). Emotional intelligence. Bantam.

Goleman, D. (2011). The Brain and Emotional Intelligence. More Than Sound.

Goleman, D., & Ekman, P. (2007). Three kinds of empathy: Cognitive, emotional, compassionate. Accedido el, 17.

Hickman, C., Smith, T., & Connors, R. (1998). The Oz principle: Getting results through individual and organizational accountability.

Hybels, B. (2016). Leading from Here to There Study Guide: Five Essential Skills. Zondervan.

Kantor, J., & Streitfeld, D. (2015). Amazon's bruising, thrilling workplace. New York Times, 16.

Kantor, J., & Streitfeld, D. (2015). Inside Amazon: Wrestling big ideas in a bruising workplace. The New York Times, 15, Q1.

Kurtzman, J., & Kurtzman, J. (1998). Thought leaders: Insights on the future of business. Jossey-Bass Publishers.

Li, L. (2014). What are the Academic Findings About Top Variables for Predicting Career Progression Potential?. Cornell University, ILR School site: http://digitalcommons.ilr.cornell.edu/student/56

Lynch, L. J., Cutro, C., & Bird, E. (2016). The Volkswagen emissions scandal.

Maddodi, S. (2019). Netflix Bigdata Analytics-The Emergence of Data Driven Recommendation.

Mayer, J. D., & Salovey, P. (1997). What is emotional intelligence. Emotional development and emotional intelligence: Educational implications, 3, 31.

Nadler, R., Carswell, J. J., & Minda, J. P. (2020). Online Mindfulness Training Increases Well-Being, Trait Emotional Intelligence, and Workplace Competency Ratings: A Randomized Waitlist-Controlled Trial. Frontiers in Psychology, 11, 255.

O'Callaghan, M., Campbell, C., Zes, D., & Landis, D. (2013). A better return on self-awareness.

Peter Hawkins & Nick Smith. (2006), API model, "Coaching, Mentoring & Organisational Consultancy"

Pressfield, S. (2014). Do the Work!: Overcome Resistance and get out of your own way. Black Irish Books.

PricewaterhouseCoopers (Firm). (2014). Adapt to survive: how better alignment between talent and opportunity can drive economic growth.

Reeves, M., & Deimler, M. (2011). Adaptability: The new competitive advantage (pp. 135-41). Harvard Business Review.

Russell, J. A., & Mehrabian, A. (1977). Evidence for a three-factor theory of emotions. Journal of research in Personality, 11(3), 273-294.

Salovey, P., & Mayer, J. D. (1990). Emotional intelligence. Imagination, cognition and personality, 9(3), 185-211.

Schwab, K., & Samans, R. (2016, January). The future of jobs report. In World Economic Forum, January. http://reports. weforum. org/future-of-jobs-2016.

Sinek, S. (2012). How great leaders inspire action. http://www.ted.com/talks/simon_sinek_how_great_leaders_inspire_action

Stichler, J. F. (2006). Emotional intelligence. Nursing for Women's Health, 10(5), 422-425.

Stone, B. (2013). The everything store: Jeff Bezos and the age of Amazon. Random House.

Work, K. I. S. Kaoru Ishikawa and TQM Landon McNaspy. Total Quality Management. Professor Lapierre. January 24, 2016.

Online references:

https://blog.dce.harvard.edu/professional-development/divergent-vs-convergent-thinking-how-strike-balance

https://innovationmanagement.se/2011/08/17/what-is-innovative-leadership/

https://www.creativehuddle.co.uk/hear-what-isnt-being-said

https://www.fastcompany.com/40522394/screw-emotional-intelligence-heres-the-real-key-to-the-future-of-work

https://www.geekwire.com/2016/amazon-radically-simplify-employee-reviews-changing-controversial-program-amid-huge-growth/

https://www.tonyrobbins.com/stories/unleash-the-power/the-key-to-success-model-the-best